TAX RESOLUTION SECRETS

DISCOVER THE EXACT METHODS USED BY TAX PROFESSIONALS TO REDUCE AND PERMANENTLY RESOLVE YOUR IRS TAX DEBTS

Jassen Bowman, EA

DEDICATION

To Ashley, for anchoring me when I was adrift in the fog.

To James, for being such an incredible mentor and friend, and constantly pushing me towards achievement.

Important Notice

While every effort has been taken to ensure that the information contained herein is accurate as of the time of publication, tax laws and regulations are constantly changing.

This book is designed to provide accurate and authoritative information in regards to the subject matter covered, but it is sold with the understanding that the publisher is not engaged in rendering legal or accounting services, and no information contained herein should be construed as legal advice.

If legal advice or other expert assistance is required, the services of a competent professional person should be sought. The publisher does not guarantee or warrant that readers who use the information provided in this publication will achieve results similar to those discussed.

CONTENTS

Acknowledgments

This book is the end of result of significant feedback from the other tax professionals that I train in the field of tax resolution. I thank you all for your comments and suggestions on the plethora of much cruder training materials I have produced for training programs. I also owe an incredible debt of gratitude to Duncan Wright and Michael Wright, for initially teaching me the ins and outs of this complex field of tax practice.

Introduction

Tax resolution is the process of developing and implementing a solution to solve an IRS problem. The optimal resolution will solve the problem permanently and settle the tax liability for the lowest amount allowed by law. You have a number of different options available to you at your disposal to resolve your tax matters with the IRS. However, most of the time, taxpayers are unaware of their rights and options. This is in spite of both guidance and dictates from Congress to the IRS to ensure that taxpayers are aware of their rights.

The options available to you for resolving your tax liability include filing unfiled tax returns, disputing the tax on technical grounds, requesting the abatement of penalties, filing bankruptcy, negotiating an Installment Agreement, negotiating an Offer in Compromise, requesting Innocent Spouse Relief, expiration of the collection statute of limitations or even being placed in Currently Not Collectible status. One of the more well known options is the Offer in Compromise program. This program allows a taxpayer who owes more than they could ever afford to pay the opportunity to settle their tax debt for fraction of what they actually owe.

The United States Congress has mandated that the IRS create a variety of programs to ensure equity within the voluntary U.S. tax assessment system. The IRS is continually challenged to this pair of objectives:

1. Ensure taxpayer compliance in collection of tax receipts to fund running the Federal Government.

2. Provide options and administer programs which give the taxpayer who has significant tax problems a fresh start.

This conflict of interest within the IRS routinely sends mixed signals to taxpayers and IRS employees. This was most clearly evident when Congress initiated a series of hearings in 1998 in response to a perception on the part of the public that the IRS was heavy handed in its approach to enforcement. These hearings resulted in a series of significant reforms. Subsequent to these hearings, a General Accountability Office report dated August 2001 indicated that this reform has been slow to take hold.

Well, this should not be surprising in an organization as massive as the IRS. The report went on to say that significant system and process deficiencies continued to impede collections and affect the accuracy of taxpayer accounts. Discussions with taxpayers, practitioners and IRS employees over many months show there's still much work to be done to achieve a balanced and equitable system.

This book will show you, without excessive "legalese" and industry jargon, the exact procedures used by tax professionals to solve their client's tax problems. With knowledge, comes power, and it is my hope that this book gives you the power to settle your IRS liabilities quickly and permanently.

CHAPTER 1

OVERVIEW OF THE IRS AND YOUR RIGHTS AS A TAXPAYER

The new mission statement of the softer, gentler IRS is to "provide America's taxpayers with top quality service by helping them understand and meet their tax responsibilities and by applying tax law with integrity and fairness to all."

This is in stark contrast to the previous mission statement which said, "The purpose of the Internal Revenue Service is to collect the proper amount of tax revenue at the least cost, serve the public by continually improving the quality of our products and services and perform in a manner warranting the highest degree of public confidence in our integrity, efficiency and fairness." Note the emphasis in the old statement which says, "To collect the proper amount of tax revenue at the least cost."

With this change in focus it is not surprising that IRS management appears to be enhancing the agency's focus on enforcement and compliance as indicated by recent IRS pronouncements and public communications.

Your Best Friend At The IRS: Taxpayer Advocate Service

The IRS Taxpayer Advocate Service was created in 1998 to assist taxpayers with the following five things:

1. Help taxpayers solve problems with the IRS and recommend changes that would prevent those problems from recurring.

2. Establish an independent channel for taxpayers who are having problems with a specific case.

3. Address the systemic problems within the IRS and identify issues that cause taxpayers problems.

4. Provide local points of contact for taxpayers.

5. Provide each state and service center with a Taxpayer Advocate.

The National Taxpayer Advocate is appointed by the Secretary of the Treasury in consultation with the IRS oversight board. The National Taxpayer Advocate serves to help the taxpayers' solve problems with the IRS when the normal processes and procedures aren't working. The Taxpayer Advocate can suspend pending collection action until the issue in question is reviewed. As a rule, the sooner that Taxpayer Advocate assistance is requested, the sooner the issue is resolved. Requesting intervention by the Taxpayer Advocate as soon as the necessary criteria are met should be done at the earliest opportunity.

An individual cannot be employed by the Taxpayer Advocate if that person was an officer or employee of IRS during the two year period ending on the date of appointment. The individual must also agree not to accept other employment within the IRS for five years following leaving the position of the Taxpayer Advocate. Annually the National Taxpayer Advocate issues a report to Congress identifying the tax areas which creating significant compliance burdens for taxpayers or the IRS and how best resolve these issues.

The Taxpayer Advocate can be your best friend, and here's why. A Taxpayer Advocate is authorized to issue a Taxpayer Assistance Order if the taxpayer is found to be suffering or about to suffer a significant hardship as a result of the way laws are being administered by the IRS. These Taxpayer Assistance Orders (TAO) are intended to provide the taxpayer with an easy and inexpensive way to resolve disputes administratively with the IRS. Their purpose is not to contest the law regarding the tax liability. The TAO procedure is also not a substitute for established administrative or judicial review procedures which you will learn more about later in this book. TAO's can be an effective tool in stopping unreasonable examination or collection activity. Often the threat of a TAO is often sufficient to cause a Revenue Agent or Revenue Officer to rethink the course of action they are considering taking against you.

Tax Resolution Resource #1

To request help from the Taxpayer Advocate Service, file Form 911 with your Local Taxpayer Advocate (LTA). To download the most current version of Form 911 and find the LTA for your area, go to www.TaxHelpHQ.com/secrets and click on "Taxpayer Advocate".

Knowing Your Rights As A Taxpayer

You have many rights as a U.S. taxpayer that you may not be aware of.

You have the right to an explanation of the audit (examination) process, your Appeals rights, and how the collection process works. Taxpayers also have the right to be represented by a representative authorized to practice before the IRS. You have the right to suspend any interview to consult with a representative, provided the interview was not arranged through the use of an administrative summons. Taxpayers have a right, with advanced notice to the IRS, to make an audio recording of any IRS interview.

Additional taxpayer's rights were added and delineated by the Taxpayer Bill of Rights in 1998. The impetus behind this was the findings which emanated from various Congressional hearings on IRS abuses. The legislation enacted a number of notable changes.

Regarding having representation, you should know that communications between clients and authorized tax practitioners are privileged as long as the communication relates to tax advice. This privilege only applies to non-criminal tax matters, however.

Interacting With IRS Employees

Manually generated correspondence received by a taxpayer from the IRS must be clearly identified with the name, phone number and employee ID number of an IRS employee whom the taxpayer may contact about the correspondence. Other correspondence or notices received by a taxpayer from the IRS must include in a prominent manner a telephone number that the taxpayer may contact. An IRS employee must give a taxpayer during a telephone or person-to-person contact the employee's telephone number and employee identifying number.

The 1998 IRS Restructuring and Reform Act list ten types of actions for which employees of the IRS can be fired. These 10 things are important for you to know as a taxpayer that is fighting to resolve your issues.

1. Willful failure to obtain the required approval signatures on documents authorizing the seizure of a home, personal belongings or business assets.

2. Providing a false statement under oath with respect to a material matter involving a taxpayer or representative.

3. With respect to a taxpayer representative or other employee of the IRS, the violation of any right under the Constitution or Federal laws such as the 1964 Civil Rights Act and the 1990 Americans With Disabilities Act.

4. Falsifying or destroying documents to conceal mistakes made by any employee with respect to a matter involving a taxpayer or representative.

5. Assault or battery on a taxpayer, a taxpayer representative or other employee of the IRS, but only if there is a criminal conviction or a final judgment by a court in a civil case with respect to the assault or battery.

6. Violations of the Internal Revenue Code of 1986, Treasury Department regulations, or IRS policies for the purpose of retaliating against or harassing a taxpayer, a representative, or another employee of the IRS.

7. Willful misuse of the provisions of Section 6103 of the Internal Revenue Code for the purpose of concealing information from a Congressional inquiry.

8. Willful failure of filing any tax return required under the Internal Revenue Code on or before the date prescribed to do so.

9. Willful understatement of their own Federal tax liability.

10. Threatening to audit a taxpayer for the purpose of extracting personal gain or benefit.

One of those frequent and frustrating aspects of working with the IRS is being transferred from person to person while trying to resolve a tax problem. Sometimes this arises as a result of not understanding the central issue or failing to accurately assess which section of the IRS is responsible for addressing the issue. However, the fault can also rest with the IRS employee or both yourself and the IRS employee. One outcome of the 1998 hearings regarding IRS practices was to significantly enhance the focus on improving customer service across all levels of the IRS. As a result, IRS employees have been encouraged to take ownership of resolving the taxpayer's problem. It will take many years for the full impact of the initiatives to take effect and be readily apparent to both practitioners and taxpayers.

Whenever you talk to any IRS employee on the phone, request the following information and write it down: Their name, their badge number, their position and title, address, date and time of the conversation, and any written notices received that you will be discussing. Request that the IRS employee provide an overview of the particular tax problem and relevant evidence to advocate their position. When trying to resolve a tax problem, it is important to agree upon next steps and the timeline, including deadlines for sending copies of documentation. Always follow-up your telephone conversation with a letter outlining the details of the call and what conclusions were reached.

Whenever you write to the IRS perform the following actions. Specify the required action to be taken by the IRS to resolve the problem, including a detailed description of the issue. Include the name, badge number and position of the relevant IRS employee. Include any copies of notices which you have received. Provide copies of all responses to such IRS notices. Provide copies of all documents supporting your position.

CHAPTER 2

TAX RESOLUTION OPTIONS

When you're trying to resolve tax matters with the IRS, you have a number of different options. Depending on your financial circumstances and the amount of your IRS back tax liability and other issues, you have several options available to you. In this chapter we will give you a brief overview of some of these options.

A Brief Word On Offers in Compromise

The Offer in Compromise is probably the most commonly known tax resolution strategy. This is what you hear about in TV commercials and radio ads, particularly when they talk about settling your tax debt for "pennies on the dollar" (a phrase which the IRS has technically banned advertisers from using). However, it is important to keep in mind that not everybody even qualifies for an Offer in Compromise, not to mention that this is only one of the many options that might be available to you. Each option must be explored in relation to the specific facts and circumstances surrounding your tax problem and then the best option can be selected and implemented. In some instances it may be necessary to employ two or more options to settle your tax obligations. Keep in mind that the ultimate goal is to solve your tax problem permanently and for the lowest amount allowed by law.

Big Option 1 – Full pay the tax owed

While seldom a popular option, sometimes you may have the ability to pay the tax outright or borrow against an existing asset, such as a cash out refinance of the equity in your home. Surprisingly, in this situation this option is usually the least costly of viable options available to you. The reason for this is simple. One, your equity and assets will usually disqualify you from benefiting from options which grant debt forgiveness. Second, until the tax debt is paid in its entirety it will continue to accrue penalties and interest. Generally, the combined penalty and interest rates that the IRS charges you are going to be significantly less than the interest rate you will pay from borrowing the money elsehwere.

Big Option 2 – Filing unfiled tax returns and replacing Substitute for Returns

When resolving a tax problem it is relatively common to have unfiled back tax returns. There are three reasons why it is necessary to file these returns and become current with your filing obligations.

1. Failure to file tax returns may be construed as a criminal act by the IRS and can be punishable by one year in jail for each year not filed. Filing unfiled tax returns brings you "current."

2. Filing unfiled returns to replace Substitute for Returns may lower your tax liability and the associated interest in penalties because the interest and penalties is calculated from the tax debt amount. A "Substitute for Return" (SFR) is when the IRS uses whatever information that they have available to them to prepare a tax return on your behalf. Now, most of the time this tax return that they prepare is not going to take into

account your expenses, your credits, and any allowable deductions. In other words, an SFR prepared by the IRS based just on the copy of your W-2 that an employer filed with the IRS is <u>not</u> going to be in your favor.

3. A settlement cannot be negotiated with the IRS until you become completely current with all filing obligations.

Big Option 3 – Dispute the tax on technical grounds

If there is a technical basis to dispute the amount of tax owed, there are a number of paths to consider, such as filing an amended return if the statute of limitations to file has not expired or filing an Offer in Compromise under Doubt as to Liability criteria. If you are currently in an audit situation and the math on the audit is simply not right then you can contest the tax on these technical grounds by fighting for the correct calculations.

Big Option 4 – Currently Not Collectible Status

If you do not have positive cash flow above the level necessary to pay your minimum living expenses or you lack sufficient equity in assets to liquidate and pay the tax, you may qualify for Currently Not Collectible status (CNC). This is most commonly seen when you are either unemployed or underemployed. In this situation, the IRS places a temporary hold on the collection of the tax owed until your financial situation improves. If over a longer period of time your situation does not improve, you may eventually become a viable Offer in Compromise candidate.

Big Option 5 – Installment Agreements

In the vast majority of cases, the IRS will accept some type of payment arrangement for past due taxes. In order to qualify for a payment plan, you must meet set criteria, which includes the following, among other things:

- You must file all past due returns.

- You must disclose all assets that you own.

- You must provide information regarding your monthly income and monthly expenses.

The difference between your monthly income and allowable expenses is the amount that the IRS will expect to receive from you under the payment plan.

Monthly payments can be expected to continue until the taxes owed are paid in full. However, it is possible to obtain a Partial Payment Installment Agreement (PPIA). A PPIA means that you'll have an Installment Agreement in place until the Statute of Limitations for collection of the tax expires. After the Statute of Limitations expires, the tax literally just goes away, along with all penalties and interest. The date on which the IRS can no longer attempt to collect the tax from you is called the Collection Statute Expiration Date (CSED).

Big Option 6 – The Offer in Compromise

The IRS Offer in Compromise program allows you to pay the IRS less than the full amount of your tax, penalties, and interest, and pay only a small amount as a full and final settlement. This program also has an option for Doubt as to Liability. In these cases you disagree with the amount of the tax assessment and this gives you a chance to file an Offer in Compromise and have your tax assessment itself reconsidered.

The Offer in Compromise program allows taxpayers to get a fresh start. In this process, all back tax liabilities are settled with the amount of the Offer in Compromise. Once the payment amount of the Offer in Compromise is fully paid off, all Federal tax liens are released. An Offer in Compromise filed based on your inability to pay the IRS looks at your current financial position, considers your ability to pay (income minus expenses), as well as your equity in assets. Based on these factors, an offer amount is determined. You can compromise all types of IRS taxes, penalties, and interest in one fell swoop. Even payroll taxes, which are often the most difficult to resolve, can be compromised. If you qualify for the Offer in Compromise program, you may be able to save thousands and thousands of dollars in tax, penalty, and interest.

Big Option 7 – Penalty Abatements

In most cases penalties make up 10-30% of your total tax obligation. A penalty abatement request can eliminate some or all of the penalties if you have reasonable cause for not paying the tax on time or paying the appropriate amount of tax. Reasonable cause includes the following: prolonged unemployment, business failure, major illness, incorrect accounting advice or bad advice from the IRS. To prevail in a penalty abatement request as in most tax matters, the burden rest with you to be able to adequately document the reasonable cause.

Big Option 8 – Discharging taxes in bankruptcy

Bankruptcy can discharge federal income tax if certain requirements are met. However, this depends upon both the type of bankruptcy and the type of tax owed. Chapter seven is the chapter of bankruptcy law that provides for the liquidation of non-exempt assets and the discharge of dischargeable debts. Chapters 11 and 13 provide for repayments of debt in whole or in part. To discharge taxes in bankruptcy, a number of criteria must be met:

1. Thirty-six months have lapsed from the tax return due date.

2. Twenty-four months have lapsed from the date the tax was assessed.

3. At least 240 days have passed since the tax was assessed and filing of bankruptcy.

4. All of your tax returns have to have been filed.

Big tax resolution option 9 – Innocent Spouse Relief

It is not uncommon to find yourself in trouble with the IRS because of your spouse or ex-spouses' actions. The IRS realizes that these situations do in fact occur. In order to help you with tax problems which are due to the actions of your spouse, the IRS has developed guidelines for you to qualify as an innocent spouse. If the taxpayer can prove that they meet these guidelines then the innocent taxpayer may not have to pay some or all the taxes caused by their spouse or ex-spouse.

Big tax resolution option 10 – Expiration of the Collection Statute

The IRS only has a limited time during which to collect back taxes from you. This time period starts on the date of the assessment of the tax and runs for 10 years. After the 10 years has lapsed, you no longer owe taxes, penalties or interest on that tax period. There are of course exceptions to this rule. You may agree in writing to allow the IRS more time to collect the tax. If you file an Offer in Compromise or if you file bankruptcy, these actions can both cause automatic extensions on the 10-year period. In these situations the amount of time for the IRS to collect the tax is extended usually by the amount of time that the action is in place.

So for example, if you file an Offer in Compromise and it takes six full months for the IRS to process your Offer in Compromise and give you a determination then the statute of limitations on collection is extended by another six months. If the IRS attempts to collect the tax obligation which is expired under the 10-year rule, the taxpayer must inform the IRS in writing that the statute of limitations has expired. Once this notification occurs the tax can be forgiven. So therefore, if you have tax liabilities that the IRS is trying to collect that are more than 10 years old, it is imperative that you calculate the exact Collection Statute Expiration Date or CSED for short and notify the IRS in writing that they are no longer allowed to collect on that tax if the date is passed the CSED.

CHAPTER 3

DETERMINING WHEN YOU NEED PROFESSIONAL ASSISTANCE

You always have the option of representing yourself in front of the IRS and that is after all, why you're reading this book. However, many times you may find dealing with the IRS to be frustrating, time consuming, intimidating, or all of the above. There are, however, many disadvantages to you representing yourself in front of the IRS:

1. You do not have the professional expertise or know what the options are or how to get the lowest settlement allowed by law.

2. Four out of every five Offers in Compromise submitted by taxpayers are rejected by the IRS. Knowing how to become one of the 20% that is accepted by the IRS can be very, very valuable.

3. Many times when you represent yourself in front of the IRS and obtain an Offer in Compromise, the amount of your Offer in Compromise is much more than is actually required by law.

4. You may end up being too frightened, frustrated or intimidated by the IRS to effectively or comfortably negotiate a settlement. Remember, IRS collections personnel are exactly that: They are professional collections agents.

5. Most taxpayers are far happier to keep their distance from the IRS and prefer to leave the sparring to their advisors. Dealing with the IRS is not always as painful as you may imagine though. In fact there some IRS officers that are reasonable and helpful, particularly when they see that you're making an offers honest effort to resolve your tax problems and pay back what you owe.

6. Unfortunately, you may slip up and inadvertently make statements that can make the problem worse, perhaps triggering an audit or even a criminal prosecution or increasing your tax liability.

7. Professionals know where to draw the line. You may sometimes make statements that can create tax liability for a business associate, your spouse or someone else.

8. Negotiating with the IRS takes valuable time away from your work and family to wrestle with your own case. Working professionals will do appreciably better paying a tax professional while they more profitably ply their own occupations.

How to Select the Best Tax Consulting Firm

When choosing a firm that will represent you before the IRS, it's important that the you know that they are dealing with a professional who is well versed in tax law and IRS procedures. IRS representation is a very complicated field with many different laws to interpret. While any attorney, CPA or Enrolled Agent may represent clients before the IRS, few are truly qualified to provide the knowledge, experience and negotiating skills needed to successfully represent you in front of the IRS.

The way I look at it is similar to a divorce, bankruptcy, or a criminal trial. Attorneys have different specializations. For example, would you hire a real estate attorney to represent you in a criminal proceeding. Or look at it in the other way, would you want a criminal defense attorney handling your divorce or bankruptcy? Most of the time, the answer is no because that is outside that attorney's area of specialization.

As a rule, a firm should have a solid tax resolution track record, which is the best objective indicator of how that firm will manage your case. Here are some key questions that you need to ask before selecting a tax resolution firm:

1. How many years has the firm been in business?

2. Is everybody that would be working on your case licensed?

3. Does the firm discuss all options available to you to resolve you tax problem?

4. What is the firm's success rate?

5. What is the firm's rating with the Better Business Bureau?

6. What is the firm's credit and financial rating with Dun & Bradstreet?

Here are some areas of concern to be careful of:

*   Beware of unlicensed telemarketers. They're paid on an incentive basis for bringing your business to their firm, and

these unlicensed sales people often have very little actual tax training, knowledge, and experience, and therefore should not be advising you.

- Be especially aware of unrealistic promises or improbable results declared by sales representatives. You want to be sure that you receive top quality work and that you get the services that you actually pay for.

- Beware of firms that charge you a fee based exclusively on the amount of money that you owe the IRS. Usually the same procedural steps are required to solve both large and small tax obligations. If the firm is quoting you a flat fee for services, ask for a breakdown of exactly what specific services every dollar of the fee quote covers.

- Ask the firm direct questions about your case. If the firm is evasive or their answer seems intentionally complex, it is possible they're trying to disguise direct answers to your questions. You deserve straightforward answers.

- Do not make emotional decisions. When you decide to hire a tax resolution specialty firm, you are seeking peace of mind that your problem will be handled and handled properly. Regardless of which firm you hire, you should feel that you are being properly taken care of and your tax problem will be solved for the lowest amount allowed by law.

Attorneys, accountants, CPA's, enrolled agents and former IRS employees may all provide valuable assistance when it comes to traditional tax accounting work. However, they may not have all of the necessary expertise, experience, and negotiating skills to permanently solve your IRS matter. Solving an IRS dispute involves day to day administrative dealings and requires the know-how to manage the maze of IRS protocols as well as having top notch negotiating skills.

How to Save on Professional Fees

The single greatest advantage of representing yourself in front of the IRS is that you'll save over the fees of a professional, and for many taxpayers this is no small matter. The amount of fees saved may be dwarfed by the actual tax settlement, however. In these situations, you might want to look at your overall financial picture to determine how much money you maybe leaving on the table if you don't have expert representation.

Tax professional's fees can range up to several hundred dollars per hour for an expert tax resolution specialist in a major city. Many tax consultants won't agree to a fixed fee to handle your case. For example, when filing an Offer in Compromise they are not able to anticipate how many hours will be required to effectively manage the case due to a multitude of unforeseen contingencies, including the reluctance on the part of the IRS to negotiate a final settlement, possible Appeals that may need to be filed, and others problems. Regardless of the fee arrangement, there's a lot you can do to keep your fees to a minimum:

1. Request monthly statements. This could warn you of overcharges or extensive fees you can't afford before they accumulate.

2. Delegate only the critical parts of your case that you can't handle yourself.

3. Cooperate. Get your financial information together quickly and in an orderly fashion. Don't make your professional chase you for the information.

4. Keep communication with your professional to a minimum. Call sparingly, get to the point, and hang up. Remember you're probably paying by the hour.

Tax Professionals to Consider

In general, you have three options of tax professionals to represent you in front of the IRS. These are attorneys, certified public accountants or enrolled agents. All three of these professionals are allowed by the IRS to directly represent taxpayers. Let's start with attorneys.

An attorney in good standing in a state bar may represent taxpayers on IRS matters. However, this doesn't mean that all lawyers are qualified to handle your IRS problem. Obviously, you need a tax attorney who's not only experienced but has an exceptional track record. An attorney inexperienced with dealing with the IRS or has a poor rating or no rating with the Better Business Bureau will likely provide very little value because they have yet to develop the feel of what the IRS will accept and do. Most tax problems are not solved in the courtroom but are resolved via administrative procedures.

It is most likely that your tax matter will be settled out of court, so an attorney's hourly fees and miscellaneous charges are often the most expensive representation alternative available to you. You will want a tax lawyer if the IRS suspects fraud, is threatening criminal prosecution, or if an appeal to tax court is likely. Ultimately, the firm's track record is the best indicator of how your case will be settled.

Next, let's talk about Certified Public Accountants. Less than 1% of all CPA's are in any way qualified to practice in the arena of tax resolution. And most CPA's have had very little exposure to dealing with IRS tax problems. As with attorneys, any CPA is permitted to handle tax resolution cases. However, that by itself is no assurance of their competence. A CPA inexperienced with negotiating or who has a poor rating or no rating with the BBB will likely provide little value because they have yet to develop, again, the feel of what the IRS will accept and what they won't.

Enrolled Agents. Enrolled agents are neither attorneys nor accountants. Enrolled agents become so either via by former employment with Internal Revenue Service or by taking a series of examinations similar to the bar exam or the CPA exam, but specific to tax matters. After passing these exams, an individual can apply to become an Enrolled Agent. An Enrolled Agent, however, that is inexperienced with tax resolution and negotiating will again provide little value. Choose an Enrolled Agent licensed directly by the IRS that is experienced in tax resolution negotiation.

How to Find a Tax Professional

Ask your professional advisors. Your accountant or attorney may not excel in tax matters, but may be able to refer you to another professional who does.

Personal Referrals

Do you have a friend or acquaintance who has gone through tax problems with good results? His or her advisor may do equally well for you. Realize that this could be a difficult matter to discuss with your friends and associates because it's similar to bankruptcy. It's not something that people commonly talk about.

Professional Associations

Your local bar association, accounting association, or state Enrolled Agents association may have a referral panel. The National Association of Enrolled Agents and the American Society of Tax Problem Solvers can also provide referrals. However, their referral does not necessarily ensure competence with IRS tax negotiation. A major thing to consider when hiring a professional tax negotiator is to consider the chemistry between you and them. You really need a professional who can offer more than just technical competency. You may need empathy and emotional support from your tax advisor. When you battle the IRS, you need a strong ally in every possible way.

Tax Resolution Resource #2

I limit my private practice to taking on three to four new clients per month. If you owe the IRS more than $50,000, I would be happy to take a look at your case and discuss whether you would be a good fit for my tax resolution firm. To request a case review, please visit www.TaxHelpHQ.com and click on "Request Case Review" to download a case review questionnaire to complete and submit. You may also reach my office by calling (970) 930-1040.

CHAPTER 4

TIME: IT'S EITHER ON YOUR SIDE OR THEIRS

(IRS STATUTES OF LIMITATIONS)

Statutes of limitations in regards to tax matters are important for you to understand because the different statutes of limitations give you different rights and responsibilities in regards to the tax matters involved. There are some statutes of limitations that work for you and there are others that can obviously work against you. It is important for you to understand these statutes of limitations when dealing with the Internal Revenue Service so that you aren't chasing a ghost or trying to make a case that can't be made.

From the government's perspective, the statute of limitations restricts your rights in many ways, such as the restriction on claiming a refund of tax you overpaid or limiting initial actions to obtain refunds.

Now, a statute of limitations may also restrict what the IRS can do against you. The statute of limitations restricts them from collecting a deficiency in tax after a certain amount of time, and also prevents the IRS from asserting either civil or criminal cases.

Either way you look at it, the statute of limitations issue provides a date of finality after which actions may not be taken by either the IRS or by you which is why it is essential for you to understand them.

Let's first look at the three-year rules. First, the IRS must assess a tax within three years after the date that you file a tax return. This three-year period also applies to penalties. Now, when is a tax return considered filed for the purposes of this rule? A return is treated as being filed on time even if it's received by the IRS after the return's due date.

Timely filing is determined by the postmark stamped on the envelope by the U.S. Postal Service or by a private delivery service. That is why whenever you send a tax return or other important items such as an Installment Agreement proposal or an Offer in Compromise application, or an Appeal, I highly recommend that you always send it by certified mail with return receipt requested.

There does not appear to be a "bright line" test to determine whether a tax return lacking a required form is a valid return. Courts will typically apply the "substantial compliance standard" to the facts of each case. This means that there must be adequate information on the return to calculate the tax liability even if a required form was omitted. The document must also indicate that it is, in fact, a tax return. An honest and reasonable attempt must be made to satisfy the tax law and you must execute the return under penalties of perjury, which is what you're doing whenever you sign the bottom of a tax return. Next time you have a tax return in front of you, take a look at what you're actually signing.

A complete tax return that lacks a specific required form such as a schedule or attachment is still sufficient to begin the statute of limitations running for assessment purposes. So for example, if you file your 1040 personal income tax return but you forget to include a Schedule E. Your income from that Schedule E is on the front page of the Form 1040. The IRS can't say that you didn't file a timely return and therefore they have to start the clock ticking on the statute of limitations for the assessment of the tax as soon as they get it.

There are special statute of limitations rules that you need to be aware of as well. When the IRS produces a Substitute for Return – which is prepared by the IRS when you don't file the tax return – this does not start running the statute of limitations for assessment. In order to start the clock running on the 3-year assessment statute of limitations, you have to file a property tax return yourself. So, if you have been notified by the IRS that they prepared the return on your behalf, it is generally advisable to file a n actual, original return as soon as possible.

A six-year statute of limitations, instead of three years, applies to returns that omit a substantial amount of income. "Substantial" means an amount of income which exceeds 25% of the gross income reported on the original tax return. The limitations period is extended to the tax payer's entire tax liability for that year, not just the omitted items.

This applies only to innocent or negligent omissions of gross income. The six-year limitations period does not apply to fraudulent omissions of gross income. If you fraudulently omit reporting income on a tax return, the tax may be assessed at any time.

Here's a bonus tip for you: The burden of proof rests with the IRS in proving that the 25% omission from income did in fact occur. The IRS cannot solely rely on the amount of unreported income asserted in the Notice of Deficiency they mail you, which they're required to send you by law

.

The Internal Revenue Code states that the IRS can assess tax or bring a suit to collect an unassessed tax at any time irregardless of any statute of limitations for some specific situations. Here are those situations:

1. You fail to file the tax return.

2. A false or fraudulent return is filed with the intent to evade the tax.

3. The tax payer attempts to defeat or evade the tax.

4. Once the tax payer files a fraudulent return, the tax payer cannot later start the running of the three-year statute of limitations period by filing an amended return to include the omitted income.

Next, let's talk about statute of limitations on collection of a tax. Once the IRS has assessed the tax within the assessment statute of limitations as discussed above, the IRS then has 10 years in which to collect the tax. There are certain events that can extend the statutory period past the 10-year mark, because they actually "stop the clock". These events include:

- filing bankruptcy

- filing certain appeal requests

- entering into litigation with the IRS

- filing an Offer in Compromise

- filing a request for an Installment Agreement

- requesting a military deferment

- filing an innocent spouse defense

With these actions, the statute of limitations is temporarily suspended while that action is being investigated.

The date of assessment is the date the Assessment Officer signs the Summary Record of Assessment. This information can be verified by obtaining an IRS account transcript called a Record of Account, which you can request from the IRS at any time. If the Summary Record of Assessment was not properly recorded, then the assessment is actually not proper. Some penalties have a different assessment date from that of the original tax. In those cases the penalty has a separate Collection Statute Expiration Date (CSED), which is the date that the 10-year period ends.

The IRS can use administrative or judicial methods to collect delinquent taxes. The IRS generally precedes administratively by levying and seizing assets that you own. If the IRS embarks upon this course of action, the levy must occur within the 10-year statute of limitations period. The IRS can also precede judicially by filing a lawsuit against you within the 10-year limitation period.

During a period of time in which an Installment Agreement request is pending with the IRS, the statute of limitations on collections is suspended for a while. The period is 30 days following a rejection of a proposed Installment Agreement or 30 days following the termination of an Installment Agreement. The statute of limitations on collections is also suspended during an Offer in Compromise investigation. During the time that the IRS is considering your Offer in Compromise, the statute of limitations clock isn't running. It is also not running for the 30 days following the rejection of an Offer in Compromise.

The situation is similar for bankruptcy. A bankruptcy petition prohibits the IRS from assessing or collecting a claim from you which arose prior to the bankruptcy petition being filed. During this period the assessment limitations period – the three- and six-year period as discussed earlier – is suspended, plus a period of 60 days after the discharge of your bankruptcy. The limitation period for collection is suspended during your bankruptcy petition period and for an additional six months after the bankruptcy is discharged.

There are times, which you'll read about later in this book, where an Appeals Officer is involved in your case. The settlement authority of an Appeals Officer is very broad. However, their primary job is to resolve the tax issue expeditiously and to weigh the costs of potential litigation for the IRS. The appeals process is one where professional negotiation skills can really come in handy. Since the appeals process relies so much upon negotiation, a high percentage of cases are resolved here. It is not uncommon for those of us that are professional tax resolution representatives to simply resolve our clients' cases in the appeals process rather than relying on a field Revenue Officer to work with us.

The biggest thing that you need to remember is that the first step in the collection process is for the IRS to actually assess the tax. Until this occurs, the IRS cannot act to collect on that tax. An assessment is simply what the IRS claims you owe. The most common forms of assessment are summary assessments and deficiency assessments.

Summary assessment will usually represent the amount reflected on a tax return that you filed, whereas a deficiency assessment can occur due to an adjustment being made to a filed tax return, such as the result of an audit, or when the IRS files a Substitute for Return.

CHAPTER 5

NASTY THINGS THE IRS CAN DO TO YOU:

LIENS, LEVIES AND WAGE GARNISHMENTS

A Notice of Federal Tax Lien (NFTL) is an encumbrance that establishes a legal claim by the government. It does not result in the physical seizure of your property. A levy, on the other hand, allows the IRS to actually seize wages, cash, or property. Levies are normally divided into two categories. The first category includes tangible, real and personal property that you own. The second category includes third parties who hold property belonging to you such as bank deposits and wages.

The first category is often referred to as a "seizure", while the second category is usually referred to as a "levy" or "garnishment". The IRS must file a lien before they can issue a levy and must place a levy upon your property before they can seize your property. Levy action is the usually the most severe collections action the IRS takes against the majority of people that owe back taxes, and it is this type of action that an IRS employee is referring to when they talk about **"enforced collection."**

Federal Tax Liens

Once the IRS makes a valid assessment against you, the IRS is required to give notice and demand for payment within 60 days by law. If you don't pay the taxes owed, a Federal Tax Lien automatically arises and attaches to property and property rights either own directly by you or acquired after the date of the tax assessment. Both Federal law and state law are relevant in determining the effect of the Federal Tax Lien against you and your property. Federal laws determine whether the tax lien has validly attached and state law aids in determining to what property the lien attaches. Under your state laws certain property may be exempt from the lien.

In general, a tax lien gives the IRS a claim against everything you own, from your home and car all the way to the rusted bicycle in your backyard. The lien also technically attaches to your wages, money in you bank accounts, your retirement accounts, and even the cash in your wallet.

A Federal Tax Lien also impacts your credit score, since it shows up on your credit report. Therefore, the tax lien can impact your ability to obtain loans, rent an apartment, and can even impact your insurance rates and ability to obtain employment if you are a job seeker.

In most cases, a tax lien will jump ahead of many other liens against your property after a 180 day period, unless a particular piece of property is used as collateral for a loan. For example, a tax lien does not jump ahead in priority position over a car loan or a first, second, or third mortgage against your home. It will, however, usually jump ahead of, say, a mechanic's lien against your home.

You may have circumstances where having the lien released would be of benefit to helping you resolve the tax situation. There are three types of lien releases available to a taxpayer that may help you resolve tax liabilities with the IRS.

Certificate of Discharge

A Certificate of Discharge (COD) is the process of removing a single piece of property from being subject to the tax lien, usually so that the property can be legally transferred. For example, if you are trying to sell your house but the presence of the lien is preventing this from occurring, then you would need to obtain a Certificate of Discharge to release the tax lien against your house.

In the vast majority of cases, the IRS will not release a lien against a particular piece of property unless they are somehow going to benefit from it. They will generally approve a Certificate of Discharge if the lien discharge will facilitate the sale of the property in such a way that the IRS will get some money out of it. In other words, releasing the lien will facilitate collection of the tax.

If the government isn't going to see any money out of releasing a piece of property from the lien, it's possible to still obtain a Certificate of Discharge if there is a valid reason. In particular, if the IRS won't be receiving any money, but getting rid of the property will free up cash flow and put you in a better financial position in regards to your income and expenses so that later on down the road you can start paying on your taxes, then the IRS will likely approve a Certificate of Discharge.

If the property in question has no significant fair market value, the COD may also be granted, but this is much more of a hit-or-miss situation.

Lien Subordination

A lien subordination is the process of moving the tax lien down a notch in the prioritization of claims against a piece of property. For example, if you own a house free and clear, and the tax lien is in first position against the house, you can't obtain a mortgage against the house. No lender in their right mind is going to loan you money against that house unless their lien is going to take first position.

The answer to this problem is the lien subordination. The IRS will usually approve the subordination of their lien against a property if the lien that will be taking first position ahead of the tax lien will result in money going to your tax liability.

In the house example, obtaining a subordination of the tax lien in order to obtain a mortgage against the house will result in cash coming from that mortgage. At closing, that cash will go directly to the IRS, the mortgage will move into first position, and the tax lien gets re-recorded in second position.

Remember, paying interest on a loan is almost always going to be cheaper than paying penalties and interest to the IRS.

There are other conditions where a lien subordination will still be approved, even if the IRS isn't going to obtain direct proceeds from doing so. For example, many trucking companies will finance their accounts receivable through a process called factoring. In factoring, a lender pays the trucking company some percentage of their accounts receivable (usually 75% to 90%) up front, and then the lender takes the responsibility of collecting on that account receivable when it's due, usually 30 to 90 days down the road. This way, the trucking company gets money now so that they can buy fuel and make payroll.

When a tax lien is filed, most factoring lenders stop funding. In that case, the trucking company suddenly loses all it's cash flow. In order to enable the funding to continue, a lien subordination can be obtained that move the tax lien to a position below the factoring lender, thereby protecting the lender's claim on those accounts receivable.

Lien Withdrawal

There are rare occasions when obtaining an outright release of the entire Federal tax lien is actually the best way to progress towards a resolution of your tax liabilities. If a case can be made that the withdrawal of the lien will facilitate payment of the tax liability, or is otherwise in the best interest of both the taxpayer and the government, then the government may be open to this.

Another case where a lien withdrawal can be applied for is when you have entered into an Installment Agreement to pay the back taxes and the agreement did not mandate that a lien be filed, particularly a payment plan where the payments are directly withdrawn from your bank account. In these cases, you can often get the lien released as long as you are current with your payments and other tax obligations.

Tax Resolution Resource #3

There are no IRS forms for requesting a lien subordination or certificate of discharge. To download template letters you can use and for addresses of where to send your application, go to www.TaxHelpHQ.com/secrets and click on "Lien Releases".

Certificate of Release of Paid or Unenforceable Lien

The IRS is required to issue a certificate of release of lien no later than 30 days after one of the following events occur:

- The tax liability is paid in full.

- The tax liability is no longer collectible. In other words, the 10-year statute of limitations on collections has expired.

- The IRS accepts the bond of a surety company or payment of all taxes owed is to be made no later than six months before the expiration of the 10-year collection statute.

- The taxpayer delivers a cashier's check to the IRS and receives a Certificate of Release of Tax Lien.

Bank Account Levies

An IRS levy is the actual action taken by the IRS to collect past due taxes. For example, the IRS can issue a bank levy to obtain your cash in savings and checking accounts or the IRS can levy your wages or accounts receivable, if you run a business.

The person, company or institution that is served the levy must comply or face their own IRS problems. For example, when the IRS issues a levy against your bank accounts, your bank must comply. The bank is required to take the funds out of your account to which the levy attaches on the day they process the levy. They must then hold those funds for 21 days and then after the 21 days, send those funds to the IRS. If they fail to do this, the IRS will come after your bank and penalize them. The additional paperwork that the bank or other company or institution is faced with to comply with the levy usually causes your relationship to suffer with the person or institution being levied.

When a financial institution receives a levy on your bank account, it cannot surrender the money until 21 calendar days after the levy has been served. This 21-day waiting period provides you the opportunity to notify the IRS and correct any errors regarding your accounts. An extension of this 21-day period may be granted by the Area Director of the IRS if there is a legitimate dispute regarding the amount of tax owed. Anytime during the 21-day waiting period the levy can be released. During these 21 days it is imperative that you exercise your appeals rights. In this case, you will want to file a CAP appeal. CAP stands for Collection Appeals Process. When you file a CAP appeal, the IRS must hear your case within five days. Please see the chapter on Appeals for more information about this process.

Levies should be avoided at all costs and are usually the result of poor communication with your Revenue Officer. When the IRS levies a bank account, the levy is only for the particular day the levy is received by the bank. As I mentioned, the bank is required to remove whatever amount of money is available in your account that day up to the maximum amount of the IRS levy and send it to the IRS after that 21 day hold period. This type of levy does not affect future deposits. So if your bank account gets levied today and all the money is taken out by the bank to be sent to the IRS 21 days later, you can make a deposit tomorrow that is not subject to that IRS levy.

An IRS wage levy is quite different. Wage levies are filed with your employer and remain in effect until the IRS notifies the employer that the wage levy has been released. Most wage levies take so much money from your paycheck that you don't have enough money to live on. In most circumstances, an IRS wage garnishment will take 70% to 80% of your entire paycheck. For most taxpayers, wage garnishments are the worst thing the IRS can do to them, and everything possible should be done to avoid this debilitating attack on your personal finances.

Personal Property Levies

The IRS's levy power is extremely broad and does not require that the IRS take you to court. The IRS can use its authority to gain possession of your property to pay any back taxes owed and all they have to do is file a notice in demand of payment, wait 10 days, then file a 30-day notice of intent to levy. After that 30 days, they can then levy. The effect of a levy is to compel you to turn property over to the IRS. Amounts that the IRS gains from a levy or garnishment are applied to your tax debt as follows:

1. The proceeds are applied to the expenses of the levy in sale.

2. Proceeds from the levy are then applied to the tax specifically relating to the levied property.

3. Proceeds are then applied to the delinquent tax liability that caused the whole situation in the first place.

4. Funds collected by a levy are considered to have been paid involuntarily. Therefore, you cannot specify to the IRS how you want those funds applied, which you are normally able to do if you make voluntary payments. This is yet another reason why levies are best avoided.

As we already mentioned, the IRS is required to notify you of its intent to levy you at least 30 days before the levy. This is done thru a notice called a Letter 1058 and states across the top of the notice, "Final Notice of Intent to Levy". When you are issued a Letter 1058 by the IRS, you have broad appeals right that allows you to appeal the proposed action. However, your appeal must be submitted within the 30 day window. If you've recently receive a final notice of intent to levy, please see the Chapter on Appeals to learn how to file a Collection Due Process appeal.

Seizures

The IRS must issue a notice of seizure to the owner of any real property (e.g. real estate) or the possessor of personal property as soon as practicable after the property is seized. This notice has the same effect as the Notice of Levy and can be delivered in person to the owner or possessor of the property or left at your home or normal place of business. Seizures must always be approved by upper IRS management. The supervisor must review your information, verify that the balance is due and affirm that a lien, levy or seizure is appropriate under the circumstances. Failure to give the proper notice will invalidate the seizure and afford you certain legal rights.

Seizures of your residence or business

The IRS is no longer really in the business of seizing homes and entire businesses. These sorts of seizures have become relatively infrequent, largely in due to the adverse publicity that the IRS has received from conducting these actions. The Taxpayer Bill of Rights prohibits the IRS from seizing real property that is used as a residence by the taxpayer for tax amounts of $5,000 or less, including penalties and interest. The Taxpayer Bill of Rights also only permits a levy or seizure on a principal residence if a judge approves of the seizure in writing. Following the 1998 Restructuring Amendments to the Internal Revenue Code, the process for seizing your home has become incredibly difficult for the IRS, which is a good thing for you.

Wage Garnishments

The IRS wage garnishment is a very powerful tool used to collect taxes owed by bringing your employer into the situation. A wage garnishment cannot only be an inconvenience and an embarrassment but it can also leave you with no money to pay your regular living expenses. Once a wage garnishment is filed with your employer, the employer is required to collect the vast majority of each of your paychecks and send that money to the IRS. As mentioned earlier, the wage garnishment will usually take 70% to 80% of your paycheck. In addition, if you receive Social Security, the IRS can take up to 15% of each and every one of your Social Security checks. The wage garnishment stays in effect until either the IRS is paid or the IRS agrees to release the garnishment.

A wage garnishment can be appealed through the Collection Appeals Program, just like a bank account levy. In addition, wage garnishments are a situation where seeking assistance from the Taxpayer Advocate can be extremely helpful.

Fair Debt Collection Practices Act

The IRS is subject to the conditions of the Fair Debt Collection Practices Act just like any other debt collector. This Act includes a number of rules controlling debt collection practices. Normally, these rules are to prevent excessive collections practices from being undertaken by collection agencies for things such as credit card debts and automobile payments. However, the Taxpayer Bill of Rights follows the Fair Debt Collection Practices Act guidelines and provides you certain rights.

For example, you cannot be contacted by a Collections Representative of the IRS outside of the hours of 8AM to 9PM, and it also prohibits harassing or abusive behavior from the IRS to you. The IRS may not communicate with you at an unusual time or place which is known or which should be known to be inconvenient to you. The IRS can also not communicate with you regarding your tax liability at your place of employment if the IRS knows or has reason to know that the your employer prohibits you from receiving such communication.

If the IRS knows that you are represented by someone who is authorized to practice before the IRS, then they can also not contact you. This provision does not apply if your power of attorney representative does not respond to the IRS within a reasonable period of time after being requested to do so. That is why it's important that if you hire professional tax resolution representation that you hire a reputable firm that's going to actually do what you pay them to do.

Chapter 6

Minimizing Your Tax Bill: It All Starts With Your Tax Returns

Penalties and interest are calculated as percentage of your tax liability. The less you owe on your actual tax returns, the less you owe overall. In a later chapter, we'll discuss the process of replacing SFR's and filing unfiled returns, but first, let's cover the tax return process itself and how to minimize your tax liability. The majority of this chapter will cover how to minimize taxes on your personal income tax return, but the end of this chapter will include a section on minimizing your liability for other tax types, particularly Form 941 employment taxes for businesses.

Your Personal Income Tax Return (1040)

There are numerous books published every tax season promising you how to keep your tax bill to an absolute minimum, and they want you to buy a new such book every year. The dirty little secret of the "annual tax savings book industry", however, is that their books are usually nothing more than heavily annotated reprintings of IRS Publication 17, which is the IRS handbook for filing a personal income tax return.

These published books, and Pub 17, walk through the entire process of preparing a tax return, including every form, schedule, and worksheet that gets attached to your Form 1040. Publication 17 is available for free from your local IRS office, or you can download a PDF from irs.gov.

My purpose in this chapter is not to go through every bit of Pub 17 and regurgitate it. As I already mentioned, there are plenty of other books out there that have already done that. In this chapter, I want to present the main ideas behind how your tax bill is computed, and what goes into minimizing it.

Income

First, let's look at the one item that has the biggest impact on your personal income tax: Your income. Income has an extremely broad definition in the Internal Revenue Code. Essentially, any time you experience a financial gain of any sort, the government considers it income, with a few limited exceptions.

Money you make from your job, a side business, or any other activity is all income. If you sell stocks, bonds, houses, or any other investments for a gain, that's considered income. If you buy a car on Craigslist, keep it for 6 months, and then sell it to somebody else on Craigslist for more than you paid for it and what you put into it for repairs, then that profit is taxable income.

If you trade services with another person and you get the better end of the deal, the monetary equivalent of that gain is also taxable as income. For example, consider a house painter and his neighbor that is an auto mechanic. The house painter agrees to repaint three rooms in his neighbor's home in exchange for a transmission overhaul on his car that would normally cost $1200. If the painter would normally charge $800 to paint those three rooms, then the painter actually got the better end of the deal and must claim the $400 difference as taxable income.

There are plenty of people that obviously ignore this rule, and you may have done it yourself. Some people even do this as a normal course of doing business, especially with the current job market and economic conditions. People that are used to getting paid in cash, just as bartenders, waiters, piano teachers, figure skating coaches, and numerous other professionals, are particularly at risk of falling into this trap.

I cannot emphasize enough the importance of properly reporting all your income, **especially** if you are already on the IRS radar. One of the most common questions that every tax professional is asked has to do with what factors increase your chances of being audited. While it is true that certain deductions and credits claimed on a tax return create a higher risk of being audited, the absolute single biggest risk factor for being audited for a tax return is *already having a tax problem*. If you're reading this book, I can only assume that you fall into this high-risk audit category. Since your audit risk is so much higher than everybody else, it behooves you to report all your income on your tax returns to avoid massive penalties, fines, and perhaps even criminal prosecution for tax evasion.

Remember, the law states that you're required to pay your fair share of tax, and not one penny more. In the world of tax geeks, I consider myself fairly aggressive when it comes to taking deductions and credits, compared so many tax practitioners that won't enter into anything that looks like a gray area. You should take each and every tax break that you're in any way, shape, or form entitled to. However, you should still report every penny of income, especially if you're already under IRS scrutiny in any way.

Adjustments

Adjustments to income are those things on the first page of a long form 1040 that are directly deducted from your income. These are deductions that everybody can take, even if you don't itemize deductions (Schedule A). Adjustments to income include things like:

- student loan interest

- moving expenses you paid for taking a job somewhere

- half of your self-employment tax

- classroom expenses paid out of pocket by teachers

- alimony you pay

- tuition and fees

- contributions to Health Savings Accounts

- contributions to some types of retirement accounts

These deductions come directly off your income, and therefore reduce a very critical number in your income tax calculation: **Adjusted Gross Income** (AGI). AGI is a term we will use frequently. Remember, it's just all your income minus the things listed above. If you paid any of these items, make sure you claim them!

Deductions

Deductions are amounts subtracted from your AGI to determine your taxable income. However, deductions, unlike allowances discussed above, are subject to minimum threshold limits. Since every person is given a "standard deduction", your itemized deductions should exceed this standard deduction in order for you to claim it. In addition, some other deductions have their own minimums before you can claim them. For example, medical expenses have to exceed 7.5% of your AGI before you can start to claim them.

Here are the most common itemized deductions to be aware of:

- medical and dental expenses that exceed 7.5% of your AGI

- state and local sales taxes you paid throughout the year

- real estate taxes

- personal property taxes (such as on cars, boats, airplanes, etc.)

- home mortgage interest and points

- mortgage insurance premiums

- interest on investments

- donations to charity

- the value of losses you suffered due to theft or natural disaster

Certain expenses are subject to what is called the 2% floor rule. Like the 7.5% rule for medical expenses indicated above, the sum of other deduction types has to exceed 2% of your AGI before you can claim them. These expenses include things such as:

- expenses you pay for your job that you are not reimbursed for, such as travel, union dues, uniforms, job-related classes, dry cleaning, etc.

- tax preparation fees

- investments expenses

- safety deposit boxes

Remember, it is the sum total of these types of expenses that have to exceed 2% of your AGI, it is NOT 2% for each individual expense. Also remember that it is the amount in excess of 2% of your AGI that you can deduct.

Don't forget, if you're able to claim any of these deductions, and you think they might add up to more than your standard deduction, then CLAIM THEM. Every deduction reduces your taxable income,and therefore your tax bill.

The standard deduction varies depending on your marital status, and the amounts generally go up every year based on inflation. If you are single or married but filing separate returns, you get the lowest standard deduction ($5,800 for 2011 tax returns). If you are single, but eligible to claim head of household status because you take care of another qualifying person (it does not have to be your own child), then you can claim the next highest standard deduction ($8,500 for 2011). If you are married and filing a joint return, you can claim the highest standard deduction ($11,600 for 2011). If you are blind and either you or yourself exceed the age of 65, you are eligible for special standard deductions.

Your total deductions, whether you take the standard deduction you qualify for or you itemize to get a bigger deduction, is very important. These deductions reduce your taxable income dollar for dollar. As will be discussed later in the chapter on Substitute For Returns, the IRS does not give you anything except the standard deduction for single people if they file a return for you, so you never want them to do this.

Exemptions

While it costs significantly more than $3,700 per year to take care of another person, Congress at least recognizes that it costs *something* to do so. Because of this, you can deduct an additional $3,700 for every other person that you can claim an exemption for. Generally, this includes yourself, your spouse, your own kids that you take care of (even if they don't live with you in some circumstances), other relatives you take care, and in some rare cases, even non-relatives you provide for.

The rules covering whom you can claim as a dependent are a bit complex, and each rule has a list of oddball exceptions. All of those rules are beyond the scope of this book, but Publication 17 has a thorough explanation, and your tax preparer can also help you determine who you can claim and who you can't.

What I would like to emphasize to you regarding dependents is this: If you even think you might be able to claim somebody, at least TRY. You may not think that you can claim an exemption for your kid niece that spent a good chunk of the year with you, but you might actually be surprised. Same with your grandparents in the nursing home. Same with your son's best friend that lived with you all year. Same thing with your kids that lived with your ex all year and you never even saw all year. Most of the rules regarding who can claim who as a dependent come down to the terms of divorce agreements, who spent the money to take care of somebody, how long they lived with you, or who simply has responsibility for the person. Again, try to claim every dependent you can, even if you think you can't – you may just be surprised. You shouldn't claim a dependent that you legally can't, but if by some weird twist of the complex rules you can claim somebody, then do it.

Like adjustments and deductions, exemptions for dependents reduce your taxable income dollar for dollar. The more exemptions you claim, the lower your tax bill is going to be.

Taxable Income and Tax

Your total income from all sources, minus your adjustments, deductions, and exemptions, equals your **taxable income**. Your taxable income is, as the term implies, the amount of your income that is actually subject to tax.

Personal income taxes in the United States are based on marginal tax rates. What this means is that your tax rate is different for different chunks of your taxable income. For example, a single person's 2011 taxable income is taxed at a rate of 10% on the first $8,500, but at a rate of 15% for any income over $8,500 but less than $34,500. The tax rate jumps again to 25% on income amounts over $34,500 but less than $83,600. This type of tax structure is also called a progressive tax, because it keeps increasing with higher income.

Since some part of your income is taxable at one tax rate, and other parts at other tax rates, your overall, combined tax percentage is going to fall somewhere between your highest and lowest marginal tax rates. This is called your **effective tax rate**. Let's take look at a quick example.

John Doe had $20,000 in taxable income in 2011, and he is single. The first $8,500 of his income is taxed ad 10%, as mentioned above, for a tax of $850 on that first chunk. The rest of his income is taxed at 15%. The remainder comes to $11,500 ($20k - $8500). That $11,500 is taxed at 15%, which comes to $1,725. Adding the two taxes together equals $2,575 in total tax. His tax divided by his taxable income equals 0.12875, or 12.875%. This percentage is John Doe's effective tax rate.

Congress changes the tax rates or the income threshold for each marginal tax rate on an annual basis. It is a large part of the annual political wrangling that goes on in Washington, D.C. between the political parties and different branches of government.

Other Taxes

Besides income taxes, there are other taxes that can be added on to your tax bill on a personal income tax return. The most common example is self-employment tax, which is the equivalent of the Social Security and Medicare taxes that an employer would withhold from your paycheck if you weren't self-employed.

Other taxes that can be added onto your Form 1040 include penalties for early withdrawal of money from retirement accounts, taxes you owe for having household help (such as a maid or nanny), and repayment of certain tax credits, such as the first time home buyer credit from previous years.

Your income tax plus these other taxes are added together to arrive at your total tax.

Tax Credits

Tax credits are important because they have a profound impact on your actual tax bill. Credits don't reduce your taxable income, but rather reduce your tax itself on a dollar for dollar basis. The tax, as calculated above from your taxable income, is some number, which is then reduced $1 for every $1 in tax credits that you are eligible for.

Tax credits are another tool of the political hornet's nest in Congress. Some tax credits are considered "sacred cows" of the system, and much heated debate erupts when a politician suggests changing or eliminating one of them. Other tax credits, such as the home energy efficiency tax credit, are the end result of years of lobbying efforts by special interest groups. Whether you agree or disagree with the political element behind a particular tax credit, the bottom line is that such credits lower your tax bill, and therefore benefit you financially if you are eligible for them.

There are two distinct types of tax credits: Refundable and non-refundable. Most tax credits are non-refundable, meaning that if the sum of these tax credits reduces your tax amount to LESS than zero, you do NOT get the difference back as a refund. Refundable credits, on the other hand, can reduce your tax amount to a negative number and the government will send you a check for the difference as a refund.

The single biggest refundable credit is the Earned Income Credit. This tax credit is the one responsible for giving several thousand dollar refunds to low income individuals that never actually pay a dime in tax. It is one of the "sacred cows" mentioned above to politicians, and is a very controversial tax credit, because it essentially serves as a wealth redistribution mechanism, literally taking money in the form of taxes to people that have higher incomes and giving it to lower income individuals that pay nothing into the system. The Earned Income Credit (EIC) can be as little as a few dollars for somebody with no children, to as much as several thousand dollars for somebody with multiple children and an AGI of less than $20,000. Again, regardless of your political stance on the issue, if you are eligible for this large tax credit, CLAIM IT!

Other tax credits, such as the Child Tax Credit (non-refundable) and the Additional Child Tax Credit (refundable), are directly related to how many eligible children you have. There is also a tax credit for childcare expenses you pay so you can work. If you sent young children to a daycare or had a babysitter or nanny, you may be eligible for this credit.

Other common tax credits we haven't mentioned already include:

- education credits for paying tuition and other fees (non-refundable)

- credit for income tax paid to a foreign government (non-refundable)

- retirement savings contribution credit (non-refundable)

- first time homebuyer credit (refundable)

- Federal fuel tax credit (refundable)

- credits for doing things to stimulate the economy (refundable)

- specially created economic stimulus credits, such as the Making Work Pay credit (refundable)

All of these credits have special rules for eligibility. Again, if you even THINK you may be eligible for one, look into, as every dollar counts. These credits are added up and then subtracted from your total tax, and may be enough to turn a tax bill into a refund.

Refund or Amount You Owe

Everything we've discussed to this point on a tax return boils down to one line: The amount you owe or the amount of your refund. By now, the math should make sense: Your total tax minus your tax credits and minus any payments you made throughout the year (such as income tax withholding from your paycheck or estimated tax payments if you're self-employed) equals some number. If that number is positive, you owe money. If it's negative, you get a refund.

Making sure you claim every adjustment, deduction, exemption, tax credit, and tax payment that you are eligible for is just as important as making sure you claim all your income. The difference, however, is that the IRS simply doesn't care if you don't claim all the deductions and credits you're allowed to – they only care that you claim all your income that you're supposed. YOU need to be the person that cares most about claiming everything that helps you, and you should make sure that your tax preparer, if you use one, also cares deeply about making sure you claim every tax benefit that you can.

Remember, if you owe the IRS money, your penalties and interest are calculated as a direct percentage of what you owe. By claiming every tax benefit you can under the law, you're not just minimizing your tax bill, you're also minimizing the penalties and interest that you have to pay. The end result of missing a few hundred dollars in student loan interest deduction, for example, can actually end up being substantially more than that in extra tax, penalties, and interest.

Bottom line: Don't be shy, claim EVERY tax benefit you're legally entitled to!

Tax Resolution Resource #4

For additional, up to date tips for minimizing your tax bill and maximizing refunds on your tax returns, please visit www.TaxHelpHQ.com/secrets and click on "Tax Returns".

Chapter 7

Understanding IRS Collections and the Resolution Process

The U.S. Internal Revenue Service is the single largest collections agency in the world. In 2010, the IRS spent over $12.5 billion and employed just under 95,000 people to collect more than $2.3 trillion in tax revenue. Of these 95,000 personnel, over 20,000 are directly involved in enforced collections action against taxpayers that owe back taxes.

Needless to say, this is a bill collector that can have a serious impact on your life, especially given the collections actions they can take that other bill collectors can't.

It is important to understand that the IRS is a slow moving bureaucracy that is highly resistant to change, and is heavily driven by forms and written procedures. This doesn't bode well when it comes to fixing your tax problem quickly, but it does provide a major benefit to working to resolve your tax problem: Their playbook is public record, and they're required to follow it.

Here in this chapter, I'm going to provide you an overview of the flow of the IRS collections process and the tax resolution process. Both processes have a very logical, linear flow. In the chapters that follow, we will discuss specific aspects of the tax resolution process, so that you can jump to the chapter and section that is specifically applicable to you, based on where you are in the linear flow of IRS collections.

Collections Starts With A Tax Deficiency

The IRS doesn't start collections activity against you simply because you file a tax return with a balance due and don't pay it. In fact, the collections process really doesn't even start when the tax assessment is made.

In all reality, the IRS collections process begins with a letter called the Statutory Notice of Deficiency (SNOD). Within the industry, we also refer to this as the "21 day letter". This letter is kicked out by a computer automatically when your "number comes up". This can actually be substantially after your tax return was filed. For individuals that file their tax return on time (by April 15th), it's not uncommon to get the SNOD two to four months after the end of tax season. For business that are behind on payroll taxes, I've seen cases where it take an entire year before the IRS kicks out the SNOD. This delay has been one of the primary things reported by the Taxpayer Advocate to Congress as a major problem within the IRS.

The SNOD is referred to as the 21-day letter because it gives you 21 days in which to pay the tax before additional penalties and interest will accrue on the tax liability. Nothing "bad" is going to happen to you during this period.

Notice of Federal Tax Lien Filing (Form 668-Y)

If you fail to pay your tax bill during the 21-day period of the SNOD, don't set up a payment plan, and don't contest the validity of the tax bill, then the next automatic step, again performed by a computer, is the filing of a Notice of Federal Tax Lien (NFTL). Under new rules issues in February 2011, the IRS will only file an actual tax lien against you in your total tax debt exceeds $10,000, including any prior years you may owe for.

As discussed earlier, a tax lien attaches to everything you own, including your wages and all your property. In addition, a tax lien is eventually indicated on your credit report, and can impact you in numerous ways, also discussed in the earlier chapter on tax liens.

Notice of Intent to Levy (Form Letter CP-504)

Approximately 30 to 45 days after the following of an actual tax lien, a computer will again kick out another notice to you. This notice will be titled "Notice of Intent to Levy" and contain a designation in the upper right or lower right corner labeled "CP-504".

When you receive a CP-504, it is important to know one major thing: It has no teeth. It is a letter required to be sent to you by law, to notify you that, because of the tax lien, the IRS has the authority to take serious collections action against, such as levies. In reality, the letter itself doesn't grant any rights to either you or the IRS, but when you receive it, it's important to mark it on the calendar, because 30 days after the CP-504, you're going to get something much, much more important.

Final Notice of Intent to Levy (Letter 1058)

Exactly 30 days after a CP-504 is issued, you're going to get another form letter from the IRS, labeled "Final Notice of Intent to Levy". In the upper right or lower right corner will be "Letter 1058".

Letter 1058 is important for two reasons:

1. It is the first opportunity you have to file an Appeal.

2. Thirty days after this letter, the IRS can actually levy you.

Here's the bottom line thing to understand about the Letter 1058: If you don't file an Appeal of this notice, the IRS *can* initiate levy action 30 days after they send this notice. In other words, you can safely ignore a lien and a CP-504, but you simply can't ignore a Letter 1058.

Does a Letter 1058 mean that the IRS *will* levy you? No, it doesn't, particularly if they don't have the information necessary to issue a levy. For example, if they don't know where you bank and don't know where you work, they can't very well issue a levy. However, if you still work at the same job that you had when you filed the tax return, the IRS knows where you work, because they received a copy of your W-2 from your employer. Also, if you have in the past given the IRS your bank account number and bank routing number in order to have a refund direct deposited, then they know where your bank is.

Whenever you receive a Letter 1058, you should file an Appeal. In order to do this, file Form 12153, *Request for Collection Due Process Appeal*. Further information about filing this appeal, called a "CDP" for short, is available in the Appeals chapter, later in this book. Normally, in my practice I will file a CDP appeal about 20 days into the 30 day window for doing so, in order to give my client as much time as possible to get their finances in order.

The Cycle Repeats

The cycle of SNOD → NFTL → CP-504 → Letter 1058 repeats itself any time you incur a new tax liability. For individual taxpayers, that means this cycle could repeat itself once per year. For a business dealing with employment taxes, this cycle could basically never end, since payroll tax returns are filed quarterly, and this cycle takes about 4 months to complete.

Revenue Officer Assignment

Your first time through this cycle, your case will exist within a division of the IRS called the Automated Collection System (ACS). ACS personnel are located at several of the largest IRS service centers, including Ogden, UT, Cincinnati, OH, and Philadelphia, PA. The majority of letters you receive from the IRS will be from one of these service centers.

Unless your collections case has special circumstances associated with it, you will usually stay assigned to ACS even if you accumulate two or three years worth of tax debt as an individual, or 3 or 4 quarters of payroll tax liability for a business. After reaching this threshold, your case will likely be assigned to a Revenue Officer. Revenue Officers (RO) are field agents that live and work in local community all over the United States. There are currently over 14,000 of these personnel working for the IRS.

An interesting thing about the current economic situation is that there are a growing number of taxpayers falling into trouble with the IRS. Because of this, the waiting line for assignment to an RO is many areas of the country is growing longer and longer. Certain taxpayers are bumped ahead of the line, depending on their circumstances. But for most taxpayers, they are waiting longer and longer, which gives them more and more time to get their finances in order and hopefully be able to work out something once they *do* get assigned to a field agent.

I've mentioned several times that there are certain circumstances that will get you assigned to a Revenue Officer much faster. Some of those circumstances include:

- your total tax debt is particularly large

- your tax liability for a particular year is quite large

- you've accumulated personal tax debt for three or more years

- you have more than 4 quarters of payroll tax liability and continue to accrue more

- you owe taxes and are not actively making Federal Tax Deposits (payroll taxes) or Estimated Tax Payments (if you're self-employed)

When you are assigned to a Revenue Officer, the course of your tax case takes a sudden shift. Having an experienced, trained human being looking at your tax case, and passing judgement on you based on what's in a file and thereby determining how they are going to handle your tax case, means a lot.

The Tax Resolution Process

Whether your case is still assigned to ACS, or if it's been assigned to a Revenue Officer, there is a fairly standard, step-by-step process by which your tax case gets resolved. Since the IRS has their own procedures that employees have to follow, you can always know what the next action from the IRS Collections division is going to be.

In general, these are the steps that you will need to follow to make progress towards a successful and permanent tax resolution:

1. Contact ACS or your Revenue Officer and negotiate a time period of 30 to 120 days in order to get your affairs in order for resolving your tax situation.

2. File appeals on any items which you are eligible to do so.

3. File all past due tax returns, including replacing SFR's.

4. Complete a Collection Information Statement, including supporting documentation, to determine your current financial condition.

5. Determine the best resolution strategy based on your financial condition.

6. Apply for and negotiate towards the chosen resolution strategy.

7. Go through the Appeals process, if necessary.

8. Apply for a penalty abatement, if necessary.

These are the same big picture steps that I follow myself when working with a client. In the following chapters, we'll take a much more in depth look at each of these steps.

Gory, Detailed Tax Resolution Process

I'm a big fan of checklists. I've used them extensively throughout my entire career, starting back in the Navy when I operated nuclear power plants on ships. When things are done with checklists, things are missed far less frequently and everything that needs to get done gets done, in the order it needs to get done.

Throughout the remainder of this book, you're going to see checklists and procedure elements that I use every day in my own practice, and also teach to other tax professionals to use when working with their clients.

What appears below are the procedural elements of each of the different tax resolution strategies discussed in further detail later in this book. The references to IRS forms won't make sense now, but they will later. For tax practitioners using this book as a reference, the steps below should be used as a guideline when working actual cases.

Tax Resolution Stages

Initially Neutral as to Resolution Strategy

1. Initial Contact: Client/Revenue Officer (within 24 hrs) / TaxPrac

2. 9297 Acquired from Revenue Officer.

3. Initial Collection action halted and 1058 Appealed ? Y/N

4. Missing Returns/SFRs Filed

5. 433 / supporting documentation (within 2 weeks)

6. Analyze current financial condition (433 / tax prep): determine final resolution strategy – this is where "tracks" below come into play

7. Client Current and Compliant

8. Request any missing information

OIC Track

OIC-1) Identification of joint vs. individual liabilities

OIC-2) Determination of Reasonable Collection Potential

OIC-3) Form 656, supporting docs & fees submitted

OIC-4) Process Examiner phase

OIC-5) Offer Examiner phase

OIC-6) OIC Appeals process

OIC-7) OIC denied

OIC-8) OIC accepted

OIC-9) OIC in monitoring status

IA Track

IA-1) Submit IA Proposal ASAP to get protection from levy action

IA-2) IA confirmed in PENDING status

IA-3) IA negotiations due to Revenue Officer info request

IA-4) IA in Appeals process

IA-5) IA denied, seeking alternate resolution

IA-6) IA accepted, 433-D signed and submitted

IA-7) IA in monitoring status

Loan-to-Pay Track

Used when equity in assets can be borrowed against to full pay the tax liability.

L-1) Loan Application Submitted

L-2) Awaiting loan determination

L-3) Loans denied; denial letters submitted to Revenue Officer

L-4) Loans denied; seeking alternate resolution

L-5) Loan accepted

L-6) Certificate of Discharge applied for

L-7) Loan closed; funds applied to liability.

L-8) Seeking secondary resolution for remaining liability

CDP Appeal Track

Used when a Collection Due Process appeal is filed on a Letter 1058.

CDP-1) 1058 Filed

CDP-2) 1058 calendared for appeal

CDP-3) CDP Appeal Filed

CDP-4) Appeals Acknowledgment Received

CDP-5) Appeals Hearing Scheduled

CDP-6) Appeals Hearing Conducted

CDP-7) CDP withdrawal

CDP-8) CDP process completed→ resolution

Penalty Abatement Track

PA-1) Penalty Abatement written & submitted

PA-2) Penalty Abatement denied

PA-3) Penalty Abatement appeals process

PA-4) Penalty Abatement denied in appeals

PA-5) Penalty Abatement Approved

PA-6) Penalty Abatement Process complete

Branch Tracks and Other Things To Consider

Outstanding 1058's with appeals rights remaining?

SFRs?

CDP filed?

1058 deadline missed – Equivalent Hearing request filed?

Uncollectible – Status 53 Eligible?

Collection Appeal Request (CAP -- Form 9423)

Chapter 8

Filing Unfiled Tax Returns and

Replacing Substitute For Returns

Earlier in this book, we discussed the importance of filing overdue tax returns and the impact of Substitute for Returns. As you may recall, Substitute for Returns (SFR) are tax returns prepared by the IRS based on the information that they have available. For example, if the only information that the IRS has available is a W-2 copy that was filed by your employer, then the IRS will file an SFR based on the wages on that W-2 and provide you with only one exemption, since they lack any other information regarding what credits and deductions you may otherwise be eligible for. You may be eligible for multiple exemptions and you may have numerous tax deductions that they don't take into account. Therefore, the SFR often results in a tax assessment that is for the maximum possible tax liability for your income level.

These assessments are often wrong. It is not uncommon for people not to file a tax return. Every year, hundreds of thousands of taxpayers fail to file their required tax return. Not filing tends to create more significant problems with the passage of time. While there may be many legitimate reasons as to why you did not file your tax returns, there are several things that you need to be aware of.

First of all, the failure to file a tax return may be construed as a criminal act by the IRS. This type of criminal act is punishable by up to one year in prison for each year of tax return that you don't file. Needless to say, it's one thing to owe the IRS money, but it's another thing to potentially lose your freedom for failure to file a tax return.

Why does the IRS care so much about you filing your tax return? Well, in all reality it's pretty simple. Because we have a voluntary compliance tax system, the IRS doesn't know how much money to charge you unless you file your tax return. That's why the IRS cares more that you file the tax return than they do about you paying the money.

Let's go back to SFR returns. These returns are filed in the best interest of the government, not in YOUR best interest. Therefore, as we already said, the only deductions you're going to see is your standard deduction and your personal exemption. You will not get credit for deductions which you may be fully legally entitled to such as exemptions for spouses, children, interest and taxes on your home, the cost of any stock or real estate sales, business expenses, and more. Regardless of what you've heard, you have the right to file your original tax return no matter how late it's filed, even if it's 10 years old.

Oftentimes, when we are working with a client and discover unfiled tax returns, pretty much everything else comes to a grinding halt until all those missing tax returns have been filed. We call this getting a client "current". By filing the missing tax returns, you will avoid the possibility of criminal prosecution. Filing original returns will replace any SFR's, which then generally lowers the tax liability. And since interest and penalties are calculated at rates that are a percentage of the tax liability, the penalties and interest will also go down.

Lastly, a final settlement cannot be negotiated with the IRS until you have filed all missing tax returns. This is true for obtaining an Offer in Compromise, a monthly payment plan, or Currently Not Collectible status. Bottom line is that the IRS wants you to file all of your tax returns regardless of your ability to pay or not pay the resulting tax liability.

Tax Resolution Resource #5

For assistance in preparing your overdue tax returns and replacing Substitute for Returns, please visit www.TaxHelpHQ.com/secrets and click on "Tax Returns".

Chapter 9

The IRS Collection Information Statement

The Collection Information Statement is a financial instrument that the IRS uses to gather information to determine your ability to pay. This is a personal or business financial statement that gathers information regarding your assets, income, expenses and various other financial items.

Keep in mind that the IRS has established standards for allowable and necessary monthly living expenses. There are certain expenses that the IRS does not allow you to claim when preparing this statement and analyzing your financial condition. For example, the IRS disallows payments on unsecured debt such as credit cards. The IRS also does not give you credit for tuition, payments, 401K contributions or charitable donations. The national standards and local standards for necessary living expenses as set by the IRS consist of food, housekeeping supplies, apparel, and personal care products and services. It also includes housing, utilities, and transportation expenses which are adjusted based on regional differences.

Taxpayers are not required to provide documentation concerning the amount of expenses categorized as national standards for your corresponding income level. However, you are required to substantiate expenses categorized as local standards or other necessary expenses. Keep in mind that the IRS considers necessary expenses to only be those that provide for the health and welfare of you and your family or that relate to the production of income. These expenses must also be reasonable in amount. Some examples of other necessary expenses that the IRS may allow include child care, dependent care for the elderly and the disabled, other taxes, health care, court-ordered payments such as child support, secured debts such as you car payments, term life insurance, disability insurance, union dues, professional association dues, and accounting and legal fees for IRS representation.

The IRS Collection Information Statement is <u>the</u> primary form from which your eligibility for the various IRS resolution programs is determined. In particular, you will be ***required*** to provide this form to the IRS whenever you are applying for:

- Currently Not Collectible Status

- Offer in Compromise

- Installment Agreement

There are actually three different versions of the Collection Information statement. In conversation, practitioners and the IRS refer to the form as just the "433", but the three versions do serve different purposes:

- Form 433-F: The short version for individual taxpayers and married couples, used by the Automated Collection System (ACS) personnel that you talk to on the phone.

- Form 433-A: The long version for individuals, married couples, and businesses that are sole proprietorships. The 433-A is used by field agents such as Revenue Officers, and also the version you should use when submitting an Offer in Compromise.

- Form 433-B: The business version, used for all purposes when the taxpayer is a business other than a sole proprietorship.

The best way to look at the Form 433 is to think of it as a loan application. If you think of it in those terms, the form suddenly makes a lot more sense. In reality, it actually IS a loan application in many regards, especially if you are applying for an Installment Agreement to make monthly payments on your tax debt.

How To Fill Out Form 433

Each of the three different versions of the form have slightly different sections and questions. However, they are obviously more alike than different, even between the individual versus business versions.

The major difference between the Form 433-A and the Form 433-B is that the Form 433-A asks for information regarding your children and other dependents, and also about your employment information.

Warning! Providing the IRS with your current employment information gives them the information they need in order to issue wage garnishments!

The other big difference between the 433-A and B is that the income and expense portion of the Form 433-A for individuals includes a column for the Revenue Officer to fill in "Allowable Expenses". At the end of this chapter, we will go through an in depth explanation of allowable expenses, IRS National Standards, and disallowed expenses.

Note: If you run a business as a sole proprietorship or are self-employed, then you should fill out Form 433-A for your business. Pages 5 and 6 of the Form 433-A contain many of the same sections as the Form 433-B regarding the business operation.

Because of the similarities between the forms, and the fact that, as indicated above, the Form 433-A does actually contain business information sections for self-employed individuals, we're going to go through each section of the IRS Form 433-B, *Collection Information Statement For Businesses*, in order to give you detailed information regarding how to fill out each section.

Section 1 - Business Information: This section is pretty straight forward.

If you don't have information regarding the incorporation date, you can obtain that information from the Articles of Organization or Articles of Incorporation, available from the Secretary of State's office where the company was formed. This date should also be in the upper right corner of each year's business tax return.

For line 3c, frequency of tax deposits, this is specifically for businesses with employees. The vast majority of small businesses are required to deposit payroll taxes on a monthly basis, but some may have a large enough payroll to be required to make semi-weekly payments.

Lines 5 and 6 have to do with online payment processing and credit cards accepted by the business. If the company doesn't sell online, mark "no" for line 4, and leave line 5 blank. If the business accepts credit cards, fill in that information on line 6.

Section 2 – Business Personnel and Contacts: *Please realize that whomever is listed as the "Person Responsible for Depositing the*

Payroll Taxes" may be investigated for the Trust Fund Recovery Penalty.

List the officers and owners of the business. Provide their Social Security numbers, home addresses, phone numbers, and what percentage of the business they own.

Section 3 – Other Financial Information:

This series of questions all require a yes/no answer. Check the appropriate box and provide the necessary explanation and other information for any "yes" answers.

For line 14, unless there is an actual event taking place, such as a major new client that will be paying the business a lot of money, mark this question as "no".

Section 4 – Business Assets & Liabilities:

My clients tend to overestimate the value of their assets. They often think in terms of what they paid for something and what it would cost to replace. However, for this section values indicated shouldn't even be Fair Market Value of the item, but actually should be the "liquidation value". Liquidation value is generally what something would sell for at auction.

The IRS wants assets information for a variety of reasons. For one, it is used in the calculation of an Offer in Compromise offer amount. Second, the IRS is looking for large value assets that you might be able to either sell or borrow money against in order to pay the IRS.

If you are still paying on any loans used to purchase the assets, be sure that information is included on the form.

Keep in mind that the Form 433-B is for a *business* – not yourself personally. Therefore, no personal assets should be listed on this form, only things actually owned by the business.

Specific line items:

#16 Bank Accounts - Indicate the name and address of the financial institution where you bank. Provide routing number (it will be nine digits), your account number and your current balance. **Warning:** Providing the IRS with your bank account information gives them the information they need in order to issues levies against your bank accounts!

#17, 18 Accounts Receivable - An Account Receivable is a customer that you did work for or provided products to, but they haven't paid you yet. Attaching a QuickBooks or similar printout is perfectly acceptable. If your business is a Federal government contractor, keep in mind that the *Federal Levy Program* will intercept any payments on your government contract and route that money to the IRS instead.

#19 Investments – Investments are things that could potentially be liquidated in order to pay the tax liability.

#20 Available Credit – List only lines of credit and credit cards that are in the name of the business, not in the name of an individual only. For credit cards, do not list trade or store cards, but only major credit cards such as Visa, Mastercard, and American Express.

#21 Real Estate: List any real estate owned by the business, how much it's worth, who the lender is, and how much is owed and the monthly payment. Also be sure to list property or commercial space that you rent, and include your lease information.

#22 Vehicles, Leased and Purchased: If it's got wheels and moves, list it here. That includes things like trailers, backhoes, airplanes, etc.

For the value, I normally use Kelly Blue Book to find values of vehicles, and will look in trade publications, eBay, and Craigslist to get an idea of values for other types of equipment. If there is a loan or lease against the vehicle, include the lender, loan balance, and monthly payment.

#23 Business Equipment: These are large business assets that are bolted down. Again, be sure to provide loan information if any equipment is leased or financed.

#24 Business Liabilities: List here other loans not mentioned elsewhere on the 433-B. These will often be bank loans, Small Business Administration loans, notes, judgments, and other debts that aren't securing equipment or real estate.

Section 5 – Monthly Income and Expenses:

This section is also very important. The difference between the expenses and income is the monthly profit of the business. This amount is used in Offer in Compromise calculations, determines eligibility for Currently Not Collectible status, and determines your monthly payment under an Installment Agreement.

In essence, this section is nothing but a shortened Profit and Loss statement. It is imperative that no expenses are omitted, so attach a Profit and Loss statement itself if necessary, or a listing of "Other" expenses for line #46.

Signature Block

Be sure to sign as a company officer by indicating your position within the company. Keep in mind also that you are signing this form under penalty of perjury.

Attachments Required

When representing a client, the single biggest impediment to obtaining a resolution of their tax liability with the IRS is obtaining all the supporting documentation that we need in order to properly work on their case. The vast majority of the time, I am inevitably submitted a Form 433-B for a client with large sections of the form blank and without significant supporting documentation.

The form itself, at the bottom, has a thorough list of what the IRS expects to see. Keep in mind that they expect copies of 3 months worth of any particular item, such as bills and statements.

Fortunately, the vast majority of the time a Revenue Officer doesn't complain about the lack of full supporting documentation. At an absolute minimum, just about every IRS Revenue Officer is going to absolutely insist upon receiving the following:

1. Copies of business bank statements for the last 3 months.

2. A Profit and Loss statement covering at least the last 3 months, but usually a Year To Date Profit and Loss.

3. At least one copy of a statement for each and every loan included on the 433-B.

In most cases, providing this minimum list of documentation will appease most Revenue Officers and Appeals Officers. If you are submitting the Form 433-B in support of an Offer in Compromise application and only submit this minimum list of supporting documentation, then you can expect a letter from the Offer in Compromise Process Examiner requesting all the information that you didn't include.

IRS National Standards and Allowable Expenses

As mentioned earlier, the income and expense section of the Collection Information Statement for individuals is quite a bit different than it is for businesses. Businesses are allowed to claim any reasonable business expense, and the Revenue Officer assigned to the case is allowed to (and often does) question any expenses that look fishy.

For individuals, though, the IRS sets very specific limits on what a household can claim as an expense, and also explicitly prohibits claiming certain expenses for collection purposes, *including expenses that are deductible or create tax credits on a tax return.* Many taxpayers are confused by this fact, and it is just one of the numerous inconsistencies across the tax code.

It should also be noted that the IRS National Standards are used by many other Federal agencies for various other purposes. The most common other purpose is that these expense guidelines are utilized by the bankruptcy courts for determining whether a bankruptcy filer ("petitioner") should be allowed to file for Chapter 7 bankruptcy or not (Chapter 7 is a liquidation of your assets and a "flushing" of your debts, whereas Chapter 13 is to set up a payment plan for several years to pay back your creditors).

Many people are shocked at how low some of the numbers are when they look at the National Standards. There are other people that are shocked, however, at how big some of the numbers are. Keep in mind that the IRS National Standards reflect the government's calculation regarding a precisely middle class existence. For example, the allowable housing expense will vary geographically, because housing is cheaper in some parts of the United States, and much, much more expensive in other parts.

However, the allowable expense for any area represents the <u>median</u> housing cost for that geographical area.

National Standards for Transportation

The IRS sets national standards for transportation, including public transit, vehicle ownership costs, and vehicle operating costs.

Public transit allowable expense: $182 per month

Vehicle ownership cost, one car: $496 per month

Vehicle ownership cost, two cars: $992 per month

The IRS also sets operating allowances for operating costs, which varies by geographical region. This allowance ranges from a low of $212 per vehicle to a max of $346 per vehicle, per month, depending upon where you live.

National Standards for Food, Clothing, etc.

The IRS sets national standards for allowable expenses for the following typical household items:

- food, including eating in and dining out

- household supplies, such as cleaning, garden, postage, etc.

- clothing, shoes, dry cleaning, tailoring, etc.

- personal care and hygiene products and services

- "miscellaneous" household expenses

The allowable expense for these categories can be claimed without documenting what you actually spend. If you spend more than this amount, then the IRS is going to insist that you document the excess spending.

The IRS national standards for the above items are based on how many people are in your household. The 2011 amounts are:

One person: $534 per month

Two people: $985 per month

Three people: $1,171 per month

Four people: $1,377 per month

For each additional person, add $262 per month

Health Care Costs

Taxpayers are also allowed to claim the actual cost of their health insurance premiums, plus $60 per month for each person in the household that is under 65 years of age, and $144 per person that is older than 65. Again, these expenses can be claimed regardless of what you actually spend. If it's more, then you will need to document what you spend.

Housing and Utilities

For most families, the money they spend on putting a roof over their head and keeping the lights on represents not only the single largest household expense, but also the one that fluctuates the most across the country.

The allowance for housing and utilities costs is also based on the number of people in the household. The range of allowable expense is quite large. For example, the range goes from a low of $671 per month for a single person in McDowell County, West Virginia, to a high of $4,041 per month for a family of five or larger in Marin County, California.

Unlike most of the other standardized expenses, you are only allowed to claim the *lesser* of the allowable expense or what you actually spend.

Summary

It is important to claim every allowable expense on your Form 433. Doing so will ultimately minimize the amount you end up paying the IRS on your back tax liabilities.

Tax Resolution Resource #6

For up to date tables of IRS National Standards and allowable expenses for your local area, go to www.TaxHelpHQ.com/secrets and click on "Allowable Expenses".

Chapter 10

Installment Agreements

An Installment Agreement is a payment plan with the IRS to resolve back taxes. An Installment Agreement is by far the most common kind of IRS tax resolution obtained by taxpayers. In the vast majority of cases, the IRS will accept a payment arrangement for past due taxes. However, there are some qualifications that you have to meet first.

As we discussed in the last chapter, you have to have filed all your tax returns. It's okay if you owe money but you've got to file your tax returns. The IRS will require that you disclose all assets that you own, including all cash, bank accounts, and even retirement accounts. You must also demonstrate to the IRS that you do not have adequate cash available to pay the IRS. You must also not have the capacity to borrow the amount owed to the IRS from other sources such as a second mortgage on your home. You must also demonstrate that you don't have the money sitting in IRA's or 401K's. Keep in mind that the total dollar amount you owe usually dictates with whom you will be negotiating for an Installment Agreement.

If you owe the IRS less than $10,000 you can obtain what is called a Guaranteed Installment Agreement. A Guaranteed Installment Agreement can be obtained without ever talking to a human being. As a matter of fact, you can obtain a Guaranteed Installment Agreement right on the Internet. You must have all your tax returns filed, however and you must propose a payment amount of at least $25 per month. If you cannot make at least to $25 per month payment, the IRS cannot by law grant you a monthly payment plan. The Guaranteed Installment Agreement is a great way to go if your tax liability is under $10,000, particularly because this type of Installment Agreement does not require financial disclosure and you are not required to fill out any financial paperwork or provide bank statements or any other information.

Now, if your tax liability is more than $10,000 but less than $25,000, then you may be eligible for what is called a Streamlined Installment Agreement. A Streamlined Installment Agreement also does not require financial disclosure via written forms and records. However, you will need to speak to an IRS Collections Representative that works in a call center called the Automated Collection System, or ACS for short. You can call ACS and obtain a Streamline Installment Agreement in most cases, within 30 or 45 minutes.

If you owe more than $25,000, chances are that you are dealing with an IRS Revenue Officer. A Revenue Officer is an IRS field collections agent. They will most likely ask you to complete a personal financial statement and if you have a business, you'll need to provide a business financial statement as well. The IRS determines allowable monthly expenses which will be matched against your actual monthly expenses. The difference between your monthly income and your allowable monthly expenses will be the amount that the IRS will require you to pay on a monthly basis.

Due to this financial review process, it often boils down to demonstrating the minimization of your income and the maximization of your allowable expenses.

When you're on an Installment Agreement, keep in mind that penalties and interest continue to accrue. This may cause you to be paying a large monthly payment to the IRS while your outstanding balance actually increases, since your payment may not even cover the monthly accrual of penalties and interest. Be careful because the IRS is most likely not going to explain this to you.

Installment Agreements are a widely used tool for tax collection. They're generally used when you're unable to pay the tax but you can pay enough each month to pay off the tax before the Collection Statute Expiration Date. If your Installment Agreement is one of the cases where the amount paid every month does not even cover the accruing interest and penalties, then you might want to consider an Offer in Compromise.

Obviously the IRS encourages you to pay what you owe as quickly as possible. If you are not able to resolve the tax debt immediately, an Installment Agreement can be a reasonable payment option. Installment Agreements allow for the full payment of the tax debt in smaller, more manageable amounts. These amounts may be seasonally adjustable. For example, if you earn your entire living in a three-month period of the year based on the nature of your business, then the IRS may accept a Installment Agreement plan where you pay little or nothing during the other nine months of the year but make large payments during the three months of the year when you are earning income.

The amount of your monthly payment will be based on the amount owed and on your ability to pay that amount within the time legally available for the IRS to collect, which is that 10-year statute of limitations we've talked about in other prior chapters. If you enter into an Installment Agreement, the IRS may ask you to sign a waiver which extends the legal maximum time for the IRS to collect. If you have an Installment Agreement already in place for a previous tax liability, you still may be able to get help. All of the amounts owed could be included in one Installment Agreement. A collection information financial statement is most likely going to have to be provided to further illustrate your financial situation.

Now, here's a kicker about Installment Agreements. In future years, if you're on an Installment Agreement and file a tax return that ends up in a refund, the refund is going to be taken by the government. You're never going to see that money. So you're not going to get all of your refund if you owe past due amounts. This can even apply to state taxes, student loans, or child support. It is not uncommon for taxpayers that are behind on child support to have the IRS seize their refund. The IRS will automatically apply refunds to whatever taxes or other items are owed. If the refund does not take care of the tax debt then your Installment Agreement will continue on until all of the terms are met.

As mentioned before, if you owe less that $25,000 to the IRS, you may be eligible for a Streamline Installment Agreement. A Streamline Installment Agreement requires that the entire amount of the tax penalties and interest to be paid in less than five years and you are generally going to be required to make even monthly payments even if you have sufficient assets to pay the tax in full. Streamline Installment Agreements are usually negotiated without the need for full financial disclosure. These installment agreements are limited to taxes on income.

Once the Installment Agreement is in place, you must file all tax returns in the future on time. If you are unable to make an Installment Agreement payment as agreed, you should immediately notify the IRS to avoid levies or wage garnishments. If you default your Installment Agreement, the IRS will generally issue a final notice of intent to levy within 30 days. Once you default on a payment plan, it is very difficult to obtain another one, although it is possible.

When you enter an Installment Agreement, the IRS is going to collect a user fee. This fee is currently a $105 fee taken out of your first payment. If you signed up to have a direct debit taken out of your bank account, they'll charge you a $52 fee instead. The user fee drops to $43 if your income is below certain U.S. Department of Health and Human Services poverty guidelines. If you qualify for the reduced user fee of $43, the IRS will automatically adjust this for you.

Keep in mind that with an Installment Agreement, interest and penalty accrual does not stop. The interest rate on a loan or a credit card is generally lower than the combination of penalties and interests imposed by the Internal Revenue Code. Therefore, if you have the ability to borrow against a credit card or a loan in order to pay off your tax liability, it may be better and cheaper for you to do that in the long run.

In order to stay current with your Installment Agreement payments, the IRS suggests doing either a payroll deduction or direct debit out of your checking account. These forms of payment help to reduce the burden of mailing payments, saves postage, helps ensure timely payments and decreases the likelihood that the agreement will default. It is not uncommon for the IRS to lose payments that you mail in. Installment Agreement payments can be made by electronic funds transfer, credit card via officialpayments.com, personal or business check, money orders and cashier's checks.

However, never send cash through the mail.

The IRS generally will still file a Notice of Federal Tax Lien to secure the government's interest in your personal property until the final payment of your Installment Agreement is made. If you enter into an Installment Agreement, the tax lien is not released until the tax liability is paid in full or the collection statute runs. Keep in mind that the Notice of Federal Tax Lien can have a negative impact on your credit rating.

Generally, IRS enforced collection actions such as levies and wage garnishments are not made while an Installment Agreement request is being considered or while it is in effect. Collection action is also not generally taken for 30 days after a request has been rejected or an Installment Agreement is terminated. Once you have an Installment Agreement in place, it is really important that you make all your payments on time. If you can't make your payments on time due to some change in your financial status, you should contact the IRS immediately. The failure to make timely payments could default the entire Installment Agreement. A defaulted Installment Agreement could subject you to enforced collection action.

By law, the IRS is required to send you an annual statement of your Installment Agreement activity. This statement must provide the amount owed at the beginning of the period, the payments posted to the account, any fees or assessments added and then the annual balance. Typically, the IRS will send this annual statement to you every July.

Besides making installment payments on time, the terms of an Installment Agreement will always dictate that you file all tax returns on time and that you make any other required tax payments due during the life of the agreement on time as well. These payments would include estimated tax payments or Federal tax deposits for payroll taxes.

Guaranteed Installment Agreements

Whenever you see tax resolution firms advertise, you'll usually see a qualifier in their ad that says something to the effect of, "If you owe the IRS at least $10,000, then give us a call." The reason for this is that if you owe the IRS less than $10,000, there is a provision in the tax code that REQUIRES them to accept your proposal to pay them in monthly installments if you meet certain requirements. In fact, you don't even need to provide them with financial statements to qualify.

To qualify for a guaranteed installment agreement, you must:

1. Owe only income tax, not any other types of tax.

2. Have properly filed and paid all tax returns during the 5 years prior to accumulating the tax debt.

3. Not be able to pay the tax immediately out of savings or other means.

4. Pay the tax fully within 3 years (e.g., the payment plan cannot exceed 36 months).

5. File and pay all tax returns on time during the period of the installment agreement.

6. Not have had an active installment agreement during the past five years.

7. Owe less than $10,000 in TAX, not including penalties and interest.

Another beautiful thing about guaranteed installment agreements is that the normal legal minimum monthly payment of $25 per month does not apply. Yes, you can actually offer payments of $10 per month, and as long as that will fully pay the debt within 36 months, they have to grant you the request!

Lastly, guaranteed installment agreements can be granted by the lowest level collections employees of the IRS without managerial approval. All you have to do is make one phone call to the Automated Collection System (ACS), wait on hold for an hour, talk to a human for 10 minutes, and you're DONE.

Do keep in mind, however, that penalties and interest continue to accrue during these - and all other - Installment Agreements, although they are guaranteed by law. Because of this, you may decide it is in your best interest to fully pay any balances due as soon as you possibly can.

To set up your guaranteed installment agreement, contact ACS at one of these numbers:

Businesses: 1-800-829-3903
Individuals: 1-800-429-7650

Streamlined Installment Agreements

While not as "easy" as a Guranteed Installment Agreement, there is another provision in the tax code for taxpayers that owe less than $25,000. A Streamlined Installment Agreement is so called because there is a very, very streamlined process for obtaining one.

These agreements also do not require managerial approval by the IRS. If you owe slightly more than $25,000, it can often be advisable to do whatever you can in order to pay the balance down to less than $25,000 so that you can qualify for the Streamlined program.

The Streamlined Installment Agreement has two very beneficial components to it. First, you are not required to file a Form 433-A or B, or provide any other financial information. Second, you can obtain this payment plan even if you otherwise have the financial means to full pay your tax liability, but simply don't want to spend the cash all at once or liquidate assets or borrow against them in order to afford the full payoff.

To qualify for a Streamlined Installement Agreement, you must:

1. Owe less than $25,000 in total TAX, not including penalties and interest.

2. Owe only income taxes if you are an individual or a business that is still operating (if your business is closed, ALL tax types are eligible, including payroll taxes).

3. Can pay off the full tax liability within 60 months or before the CSED.

As with all Installment Agreements, you must make all your payments on time and file all tax returns on time, paid in full, during the course of the payment plan.

If you enter into a Streamline Installment Agreement *before* a tax lien is filed, you can often avoid the filing of the Notice of Federal Tax Lien.

As always, penalties and interest still build up during the course of making payments on this payment plan.

Partial Payment Installment Agreements

A Partial Payment Installment Agreement (PPIA) is a payment plan where you will be making payments until the Collection Statute Expiration Date, but the entire tax liability won't be paid off. In many ways, this is similar to one of the payment options for the Offer in Compromise program. This option did not used to exist for taxpayer, but was created as an option under the American Jobs Creation Act of 2004.

Under IRS regulation, the agency will not normally ask a taxpayer to sign a document authorizing the extension of the CSED when an Installment Agreement is granted. The lone exception to this regulation is a PPIA, but even this is only in certain situation.

When requesting this type of payment plan, the IRS will closely scrutinize your assets. If you own anything that you can borrow against or sell and put that money towards the tax liability, the IRS is going to *require* that you at least attempt to sell or borrow against those assets.

PPIA's will require extensive financial documentation, including a full Form 433 and complete supporting documentation. Also, a Notice of Federal Tax Lien will definitely be filed against you if it hasn't been already.

If you are a candidate for a PPIA, and lack significant equity in your assets, then you may also want to consider applying for an Offer in Compromise. You may end up paying less under one program or the other, so they are both worth considering under these circumstances.

Chapter 11

Delayed Collection and

Currently Not Collectible Status

IRS policy states that whenever a taxpayer raises a question or presents information creating reasonable doubt as to the validity of a tax liability, reasonable forbearance will be exercised with respect to collection efforts as long as the interests of the government are not jeopardized. Now, this doesn't mean that your tax debt is going to be forgiven, or that the tax lien is going to be released, or that interest and late payment penalties don't continue to accrue. What it does is that it suspends collection action until you have the ability to actually pay the tax.

A very powerful tool for getting the IRS off your back is Currently Not Collectible (CNC) status. The IRS recognizes that you maybe in a financial condition that renders you unable to pay anything on your taxes. When I represent taxpayers that are either insolvent or are having major cash flow issues, the Currently Not Collectible Status is the option that we attempt to obtain most often.

If you have negligible assets subject to levy enforcement by the IRS and you have no income beyond what is absolutely necessary for you to live, the IRS may determine that your liability is currently uncollectible. Currently Not Collectible status defers collection action under the undue hardship rule. If you are one of these uncollectible cases, the Revenue Officer assigned to your case will remove your case from active inventory until your financial condition improves. Currently Not Collectible Status is generally maintained for about one year. There are many reasons the IRS may close your case as uncollectible. These include:

1. The creation of undo hardship for you, leaving you unable to meet necessary living expenses.

2. The inability to locate any of your assets.

3. The inability to contact you.

4. You die with no significant estate left behind.

5. Bankruptcy or suspension of business activities with no remaining assets.

6. Special circumstances such as tax accounts of military personnel serving in a combat zone.

Do keep in mind that if you are in Currently Not Collectible Status, penalties and interest will continue to accrue on your tax liabilities.

Before closing your case for the reason of undue hardship, I guarantee that the IRS will request a financial statement from you so that they can review your finances. The review is similar to the review for an Installment Agreement request and both of these items are similar to a mortgage application. You will be required to provide similar financial documentation such as bank statements, copies of mortgage statements and car payments, pay stubs, etc. If your assets are negligible and your net disposable income is negligible, you'll most likely to be able to obtain a CNC status.

The IRS will periodically re-examine your finances to see if your financial condition has improved to the point that some payment can be demanded. This financial review will occur about once a year and you must then complete a new financial statement. The IRS may question you by phone or in person about your updated financial information or they may simply send you the form and request that you return it by mail.

As with all information you give the IRS, make sure that what you say is absolutely truthful. The IRS may also monitor your financial condition by computerized review of your tax returns. For example, the IRS computers may flag your return if your reported gross income exceeds some pre-established amount. Remember, the IRS only has 10 years from the date of assessment to collect delinquent taxes; once the statute expires, so does your liability.

Millions of Americans have remained in CNC for years and completely avoided having to pay their back taxes. Obviously, these folks could not title assets in their own name or have significant income available for IRS levy. Still, many of these uncollectible cases enjoyed relatively comfortable lifestyles. If you maintain no assets in your own name, you have a small income, and expect your financial situation to continue, then remaining in CNC status may be your most practical remedy. However, if you do not intend on remaining uncollectible until the statute of limitations expires or you don't want the tax liability hanging over your head, then you may want to consider an Offer in Compromise while your financial situation isn't so great.

Taxpayers have been able to get Offers in Compromise accepted while being in CNC for literally just a few hundred dollars when they've been able to borrow the money from friends or family members strictly for purposes of settling the tax debt under the Offer in Compromise program.

Your Revenue Officer has the authority to place you into CNC. While declaring your accounts non-collectible does not eliminate the assessment, it does stop current efforts to collect the tax, and stopping enforced collection action is typically your overall objective. Collection can resume anytime before the end of the 10 year statute of limitations expires.

The decision by the IRS to place an account in Non-Collectible Status is generally based upon the information on your financial statement and this information must be no more than 12 months old. The IRS can place you in Non-Collectible Status even when you're financial statement reflects assets or income which can be levied as long as the collection of the delinquent taxes would prevent you from affording necessary living expenses.

Remember, your situation is unique. Factors such as health and age are considerable by the IRS. If you can make monthly payments of at least $25 per month, the IRS will most likely require to you enter an Installment Agreement instead. If you owe more than $10,000 and are placed in a Non-Collectible Status, a tax lien will be filed against you if it hasn't been already.

Chapter 12

Offer in Compromise Program

Whenever you hear the phrase "pennies on the dollar" in relation to tax resolution, you are hearing a reference to the Offer in Compromise (OIC) program.

The OIC program is intended to give taxpayer's without the financial means to pay their tax debt to pay whatever they have, and then start over. In many ways, an OIC is akin to a bankruptcy filing on taxes only. The major difference, however, is that an OIC is an administrative proceeding, rather than a court proceeding.

An Offer in Compromise application will require complete financial disclosure. In other words, a full and accurate Form 433-A or Form 433-B will be required, along with *complete* supporting documentation. Because the government is going to accept less money for the tax debt than what you owe, they are going to go to great lengths to make sure that you actually qualify.

You should note that almost 80% of all Offers in Compromise are ultimately rejected by the IRS, either via the Offer process itself, or in Appeals. The biggest reason that Offers are rejected is because the applicant simply wasn't eligible for the program.

Some taxpayers file an OIC simply to "buy time" to figure something else out, since the process normally takes 6 to 9 months for an Offer application to be processed and denied, including Appeals. While this may be a worthwhile strategy for you, you should note the CSED is extended day-for-day while your Offer is in process, and for 30 days after it is ultimately denied.

Eligibility

Your eligibility to settle for less than what you owe is directly related to your offer amount (see "Offer Calculation"). If your offer amount is equal to or greater than the minimum amount calculated using the IRS formula, then you may be eligible to file an Offer in Compromise.

Like other resolution options, the IRS also requires that you:

- have filed all past due tax returns

- are not currently generating new tax liabilities

- agree to properly file and pay on all tax returns, on time, for the next 5 years

- agree to let the IRS keep any tax refunds you would otherwise be due during the time you are paying on the OIC

Failure to abide by these rules will either result in rejection of your offer, or default of your offer agreement and reinstatement of any tax liabilities that were eliminated.

Payment Options

In addition to a $150 application fee, you are required to make payments on the Offer in Compromise unless you meet low income qualification guidelines for an exception to this rule.

The first payment option is used when you will pay the entire amount of your settlement offer in 5 monthly payments or less. If you use this option, you may pay the entire offer amount when submitting your application, or include a minimum 20% deposit (non-refundable!) and take up to a maximum of 5 more monthly payments to pay off your offer. Using this payment option provides the benefit of not being required to make regular payments on your Offer while it is being processed. Using this option also generally results in paying the smallest possible Offer amount.

The second payment option requires you to make regular payments on your Offer in Compromise while the IRS is considering it. These payments are non-refundable, and the first payment needs to be included with your offer application. The second payment option takes longer than 5 months to pay off. Under the new OIC rules, you can essentially take as long as you want to make these payments.

Older OIC guidelines had three payment options: The 5-month option now called Payment Option 1 (formerly called "Lump Sum Cash Offer"), another option with a 24 month payment limit (formerly called the "Short Term Periodic Payment Offer"), and a third option allowing up to 60 months or until your CSED, whichever was longer. The new payment options get rid of the confusing names and combine two longer old options.

Regardless of the payment option you use, your payments must add up to the total offer amount, and your offer amount must be at least your Reasonable Collection Potential (RCP), discussed next.

Keep in mind that penalties and interest continue to build on your tax liability while you make Offer payments, even though ultimately those penalties and interest go away when the Offer is paid off and settled. If you default on your OIC, however, those built up penalties and interested are added back on to your balance and you will be liable for it.

Offer Calculation

Many unlicensed tax resolution salespeople, either through ignorance or simply gross incompetence, will tell everybody that they talk to that they qualify for an OIC, and that the Offer amount is some percentage of what they owe.

In addition to this horrifically unethical practice, many tax resolution firms will also only tout their most successful OIC applications, showing you that they did indeed get 1.2 cents on the dollar for one client, and 4 cents on the dollar for another client, all while failing to inform you that:

a. Most of their OIC applications for clients were outright rejected, and

b. of those that were accepted, it was usually only for 50 or 75 cents on the dollar.

The Offer amount is the single most important part of a successful OIC application. Calculating the OIC offer amount is extremely formulaic, and requires a complete and accurate Form 433 to be filled out. The IRS goes through an extensive investigation phase to verify information on your Form 433, looking for other assets you own and income you failed to disclose. The IRS looks at various public records sources, and may even pull a credit report to verify what you've told them (this action doesn't require your direct authorization to the IRS under Federal law).

Within the IRS booklet containing the OIC application, there are versions of the Form 433-A and Form 433-B that are modified slightly for OIC purposes. If you use the PDF version of the booklet (search for "IRS Form 656B"), the calculations are actually carried forward for you to the lines that determine your Offer amount.

The entire purpose of these calculations is to arrive at what the IRS calls your "Reasonable Collection Potential", or RCP. The RCP is the sum of the net worth of your assets plus all of your disposable income for the next 4 or 5 years. In other words:

Settlement Amount = (monthly disposable income x a number of months) + the net realizable equity in the taxpayer's assets)

Disposable income is monthly income minus allowable monthly expenses. It is important to recognize that the IRS will not allow all expenses that you may actually have. Common disallowed expenses are college tuition payments for a dependent and credit card payments (disallowed since they represent unsecured debt). For more information on this topic, refer to the chapter on IRS Collection Information Statements.

The number of months over which disposable income must be calculated into the offer amount is based on the smaller of the number of months remaining until the Collection Statute Expiration Date (CSED) for the tax debt OR either 48 or 60 months, depending on the payment option for the OIC which the applicant is selecting.

"Net realizable equity in assets" is the quick sale value of the asset (often 80% of Fair Market Value (FMV)) minus any liabilities which are secured by the asset (e.g., a loan). As an example, if a taxpayer has a home worth $100,000 and owes $50,000 on the home, the IRS will calculate the net realizable equity in the asset as follows: ($100,000 x .80) - $50,000 = $30,000. The IRS expects, in this example, that the $30,000 will be included in the Offer amount.

Based on this explanation of how RCP is determined, and understanding that RCP is your minimum offer amount, I hope it is apparent as to why the IRS rejects so many OIC applications. In reality, the best OIC candidates are folks that have very little in the way of assets, and no disposable income. The best OIC candidates often tend to be unemployed and broke.

Application Process – What To Expect

When you file an OIC, a Process Examiner will look over your paperwork to make sure that the offer is "processable", meaning that you met all the administrative requirements to be eligible, properly filled out the forms, crossed your t's and dotted your i's, filled out a complete Form 433, and have filed all your tax returns.

If your Offer is deemed to be not processable, it will be returned to you with a letter from the Process Examiner explaining what you need to correct, and to resubmit your offer with those corrections.

If considered processable, an Offer Examiner will then be assigned to actually review the merits and financial aspects of your application. This is the person that verifies assets, orders credit reports, and basically gets very up close and personal regarding every aspect of your financial situation or the financial health of your business.

The Offer Examiner will usually provide you the opportunity to address any inconsistencies they discover in their findings, and to argue on your own behalf for the inclusion or exclusion of certain assets or expenses. More often than not, this is the phase where having a professional representative comes in handy the most, to handle these negotiations for you.

Once the Offer Examiner has all the information they need to either accept or reject your Offer, they will do so, and send you a letter explaining why.

Keep in mind that for Payment Option 2, you must continue to make monthly payments on your OIC while this review process is going on. If you fail to do so, your offer will automatically be rejected, and the IRS will keep the money you did pay and apply it to your tax liability as they see fit.

Appeals

If your OIC is rejected, you have the right to know why, and also the right to Appeal this decision. More often than not, a dispute over including an asset or expense item will be the argument you take to Appeals. Appeals Officers have the authority to accept or reject an OIC based on their own findings, rather than the findings of the Offer Examiner.

For more information regarding dealing with Appeals in general, see the Appeals chapter, later in this book.

Chapter 13

Reducing IRS Penalties With

Reasonable Cause Penalty Abatements

There are a lot of common misconceptions surrounding the abatement (removal) of IRS penalties and interest.

First of all, it is important for anybody that owes the IRS money to understand that you will not have interest charges removed. If somebody is trying to sell you on their tax relief services and they tell you that they can have the amount of interest on your tax account reduced or eliminated, they're lying. The provisions within the U.S. tax code for eliminating interest charges on back taxes are extremely limited and extremely specific, and if you owe the money but just simply couldn't or didn't pay it, you DO NOT qualify.

The second thing to understand is that the removal of any penalties is extremely formulaic. You must meet one of the reasonable cause criteria outlined by the Internal Revenue Code. Fortunately, these reasonable cause criteria are much broader and more applicable to more people and businesses than are the criteria for interest abatement. Some of the possible reasonable cause criteria include death or illness in the family, loss of records, and receiving bad advice from a CPA.

It is important to note that the two most common causes for accrual of a tax liability are not considered reasonable cause by the IRS, and most often you will not be able to have penalties reduced for these two reasons. These reasons are:

1. Ignorance of filing or deposit requirements

2. Cash flow problems that leave you without enough money to pay the tax when due

Under special circumstances, the IRS will grant penalty relief due to economic hardship, but it is a hard case to prove and tends to be a longer, more drawn out process through the Appeals division. The granting of this sort of penalty relief can also depend upon which Circuit Court of Appeals district you live in, since different case law has been interpreted in a different court jurisdictions.

Above all, just remember that you can get penalties abated, if you have a good reason that was beyond your control and that can be backed up with proper documentation. And as far as interest charges go – forget about it, the IRS is not going to let you off the hook for those if you actually do owe the tax.

One of the biggest things I am adamant about is correcting the myths, lies, and half-truths perpetuated by unlicensed tax resolution salespeople, and the IRS penalty abatement is one of the things least understood and grossly over-hyped by salespeople in our industry.

The "we can remove interest charges" lie, as mentioned at the start of this chapter, is one of the biggest lies that tax resolution sales people tell their propsects.

There are two, and precisely two, instances in which interest is reduced:

1. An IRS employee gives you false information, which you acted on and resulted in the interest. This is one reason why all IRS correspondence should be conducted and followed up in writing.

2. Since interest is calculated based on the tax liability, if an amended return is filed and the tax itself is lowered, then the interest is also reduced.

Reasonable Cause Criteria

Now, on to penalties. The IRS charges dozens of different types of penalties, but the three that we most commonly talk about are the late filing penalty, the late payment penalty, and the penalty for not making Federal Tax Deposits. These three penalties combined can add a whopping 65% to your total IRS bill. If your tax debt is more than two years old, you've maxed out all these penalties, and therefore over half your total debt is penalties.

The IRS does actually have a compassionate side, and it's generally found in the penalty abatement process. Penalty abatement applications can also be appealed if initially denied, so you can always get a second set of eyeballs on the issue. The thing to keep in mind is that the IRS has very strict guidelines for granting penalty abatements, and these guidelines are referred to as "reasonable cause criteria".

As mentioned earlier, "we didn't have the money" is NOT a reasonable cause criteria. A drop in revenue, by itself, is insufficient argument for obtaining penalty relief. Any request for penalty abatement simply citing the economic recession will be immediately denied.

Why is this? Here is the IRS' logic: You made the money, and should have paid the taxes at the time on that money. If you are self-employed and receive a check, then you HAD the money, you simply didn't give the IRS their chunk of it. Same goes with payroll taxes for businesses, particularly the trust fund taxes (money you withhold from employee paychecks for income tax and

Medicare/Social Security): If you had the expectation to pay some amount of wage, then you theoretically HAD the money sitting somewhere to pay that person, and should have withheld it and turned it over to the IRS. If you couldn't cover the taxes, you shouldn't have had the employee and should have laid people off or cut back their hours.

There are ways to argue around this, and we have done so very successfully, but there has to be some other circumstance. For example, you had the money to pay the tax, but paying the tax instead of something else would have created an "undue hardship".

Examples of "undue hardship" could include a large medical expense that unpaid would have left a condition untreated, or a court ordered payment that, if missed, would have resulted in other legal consequences, or a bill such as a large automobile repair which would have left you unable to get to work and resulted in job loss.

These arguments are difficult to make and require significantly more work than standard reasonable cause criteria applications, but they CAN be won, especially in the Appeals process.

The primary IRS penalty abatement reasonable cause criteria center around natural disasters, loss or destruction of vital business records, bad advice from the IRS or an accounting professional, criminal activity, medical issues, substance abuse problems, and other serious circumstances.

A couple years ago I developed a standard list of questions to ask clients to assist me in preparing their penalty abatement. This list of questions should be given some serious thought before requesting penalty abatement, as you are more likely to get what you want if your request covers one of these areas:

- Were any financial records lost or destroyed?

- Was there any transition in your business that lead to the failure to pay taxes, such as a change of ownership?

- Was there a death or serious illness that directly affected your ability to work or impacted the operation of your business?

- Were you the victim of any embezzlement of funds, theft of valuable property, or identity theft?

- Were there any alcohol or drug abuse issues that affected your business or your personal wage earning capability?

- Was there a natural disaster that impacted you or your business?

- Did you rely on the advice of a CPA or IRS employee in making tax decisions?

- Were there any circumstances that created substantial financial hardship, to the point where either yourself or your business was close to going bankrupt?

These questions cover all of the IRS reasonable cause criteria to one extent or another, so finding an answer to your personal or business situation that covers one or more of these questions is the key to a successful penalty abatement application.

Writing Your Penalty Abatement Request

You can use Form 843, *Claim for Refund and Request for Abatement* to apply for relief from penalties. However, as a tax practitioner, I never have, not even once. The reason is simply because the form only has room for about two sentences in order to explain WHY you are requesting the penalties to be removed. Therefore, you're going to end up writing a lengthy letter anyway that gets attached to the Form 843. Because of this, I simply write a letter for my clients that includes all the same information as the Form 843. My typical penalty abatement letter is 3 to 5 pages long, and some are even longer.

The format of a penalty abatement letter is fairly straightforward. When requesting a penalty abatement, I suggest the following format:

1. Indicate the particular penalty types, tax periods, and penalty amounts that you are requesting to be reduced or removed.

2. Include a very brief introduction about who you are, where you live, your family size, and what you do. For a business, give a very brief description of your business, what it does, and how it does it.

3. Provide the background story to the event that caused the tax bills to go unpaid. Be sure to include very specific details, including names, dates, places, events, etc.

4. After explaining why the taxes weren't paid, explain what actions you took to correct the situation, including an explanation regarding the length of time it took to get the tax situation addressed.

5. For business taxes, explain why other business expenses were paid when the taxes were not.

6. Explain the current state of affairs, including the current status of your personal or business finances, and also the status of meeting your current tax obligations and how you've addressed the back tax liabilities

7. Sign your request under penalties of perjury.

Where To Send Penalty Abatement Requests

If you have or recently had a Revenue Officer assigned to you, send your penalty abatement request to that Revenue Officer.

If you do not have a Revenue Officer: Most of your IRS notices most likely come from one particular IRS service center. Make note of the address of that IRS center, and mail your request their to the attention of "Service Center Penalty Appeals Coordinator".

Penalty Abatement Review Process

Whether it is a Revenue Officer or the service center coordinator that reviews your request, they will make a determination regarding whether they believe your request meets reasonable cause criteria.

If it is determined that your application meets reasonable cause criteria, the person reviewing your request will recommend removal of penalties for certain types and period, based on your circumstances. This recommendation will then be forwarded to a manager for final approval.

If your request is denied, you will be told so in writing. You are entitled to know the exact reason that your request was denied. If you are not supplied with this reason in the initial rejection letter, then you should call or write to that person to request it.

All penalty abatement denials have appeals rights. Requesting appeals consideration of your penalty abatement is covered in the next chapter.

Tax Resolution Resource #7

If you would like a penalty abatement template letter you can use that has a proven track record of successfully obtaining massive reductions in penalties , go to www.TaxHelpHQ.com/secrets and click on "Penalty Abatements".

Chapter 14

Working With IRS Appeals

The Appeals division is one of the IRS' best kept secrets. In my experience, Appeals personnel appear to be under less pressure to collect tax revenue than Revenue Officers, probably due to different criteria for personnel reviews. In addition, Appeals personnel are simply more pleasant to deal with in general, usually lacking the snappy attitude and air of arrogance that is unfortunately common amongst Revenue Officers.

The primary function of Appeals is to offer a "fresh look" at cases. Their functional mandate from on high is, effectively, to prevent cases from going to court, thus saving the government the expense of litigation. Appeals, however, is still an administrative function, and is *not* a court in any way itself.

Appeals works in a very formulaic manner, just like any other IRS division. When you file any sort of IRS appeal, you'll receive a letter notifying you that your case has been assigned to a Settlement Officer (SO). Sometimes, this first letter will include your hearing date, sometimes it won't.

The initial contact from appeals via mail will usually include a request for financial documentation if this information wasn't already in your file when it was passed to Appeals from Collections. If your Appeal in any way mentions a "resolution alternative", then you will be requested to provide the financial documentation necessary to reach that resolution alternative, such as an Installment Agreement, CNC, or Offer in Compromise.

While it would seem contrary to the fundamental function of the Collections division, well over half of all Installment Agreements I ultimately negotiate for clients are created by a Settlement Officer within the Appeals division. They provide an excellent opportunity to resolve your tax case and prevent it from going back to Collections. Appeals itself doesn't carry out enforced collections activity such as issuing liens, levies, and seizures, but if they kick your case back to a Revenue Officer, such action is very likely to follow pretty soon.

While there are a number of different actions you can Appeal, here are the primary ones that most taxpayers should take note of:

- Collection Due Process (CDP)

- Collection Appeals Program (CAP)

- Trust Fund Recovery Penalty Assessment Appeals

- Penalty Abatement Denial Appeals

Each of these programs has specific rules, requirements, and procedures. We will take a look at each of them in greater detail from this perspective.

Collection Due Process Appeals

Collection Due Process (CDP) appeals are filed when proposed enforced collection activity is unwarranted because you believe there is a better alternative for resolving the tax situation. In other words, a CDP is what you file when you disagree with proposed levy action. When you receive a Letter 1058, Final Notice of Intent to Levy, a CDP appeal is your response to that notice.

Technically, a CDP appeal can be filed under any of the following circumstances:

- a Notice of Federal Tax Lien is filed against you

- a Final Notice of Intent to levy is received

- a Notice of Jeopardy Levy is received

- your state tax refund is taken by the IRS

You have a window of 30 days from when one of the actions above is taken against you in order to file a CDP. You file a CDP using IRS Form 12153, and it is filed with the Revenue Officer, service center, or other division from which you received the notice.

If you request a CDP hearing on time, it will usually stop the proposed levy action. Because the Appeals division is fairly overwhelmed these days, and CDP appeals have a lower priority than many other appeals types, it could actually be several months before your case is assigned to a Settlement Officer and you obtain a hearing. In other words, filing a CDP appeal is a great way to "buy time" to get your financial affairs in order for obtaining a payment plan.

It should be noted that when you file a CDP request, the statute of limitation that the IRS has for collecting the tax (CSED) is extended day for day while you're awaiting a hearing. Therefore, filing a CDP on a tax that is about to expire may not be the best idea.

If you do not file a CDP on time, you can request what is called an "Equivalent Hearing", and Appeals will still hear your case. However, you do not receive the protection from levy action while awaiting an Equivalent Hearing, and the CSED is *not* extended (which can sometimes be a good thing).

When working with clients and filing a CDP, I will also indicate a collection alternative on the form, and include further explanation such as this on the "other" line of the form:

> "Taxpayer intends to resolve the outstanding liability through an appropriate Installment Agreement. Since a reasonable collection alternative exists, levy action should not take place."

By using this type of language, I'm explicitly stating a case for Appeals to consider.

When you receive your notice from Appeals stating that they have received your request, be sure to look for the following items in particular on that notice:

- your hearing date and time, if scheduled

- whether you are calling them, or they are calling you

- any requests for financial information (Form 433) and the deadline they set for getting that information

Deadlines and appointments set by Appeals are extremely important to keep. If you miss a deadline or a hearing, you won't get another one. If the hearing date is inconvenient because of your work schedule or some other reason, it's OK to call and request another time, they will usually accommodate such a reasonable request.

The financial information that you provide should correlate with your alternative collection option. For example, if you have requested an Installment Agreement, then your Form 433 and supporting documentation should reflect the monthly payment you believe you can pay. Similarly, if you are requesting CNC status, then your financial information should essentially indicate that you are broke and make insufficient income to pay basic living expenses.

If Appeals agrees to grant you a resolution option, then they will draft the agreement and send it to you to sign. As with all paperwork from the IRS, read it very carefully to be sure you are signing what you think you are signing. If unsure, have it reviewed by a competent tax professional that can advise you about what the agreement contains.

Collection Appeals Program

The Collection Appeals Program (CAP) is an interesting critter within the IRS world. CAP is an incredibly time-sensitive program within the IRS, and forces the agency to break most of the speed limits that inherently exist in a bureaucracy. When the CAP program was created by Congress in 1998, the legislation with intentionally worded to create this urgency of action, in order to give provide solutions to taxpayer's issues in a timely manner.

A CAP hearing is requested by filing IRS Form 9423, and is available for the following actions:

- filing of a Federal Tax Lien

- denial of a lien discharge or subordination,

- an actual levy

- a seizure

- Denial of an Installment Agreement request

- Termination of an active Installment Agreement

Whenever any of these actions takes place, you can file a collection appeal request with the office that issued the action. Many times, this will be directly with your Revenue Officer. The beauty of the CAP program is that the IRS is required to give you a hearing between with a manager of the department that filed the action against you within two business days of you filing the request.

Under the tax code, you are entitled to a stay of enforcement when you file a CAP request. If you have a manager conference first, before filing Form 9423, you have two days in which to file it after the manager hearing in order to receive this protection against further levy action. If you are appealing the denial of an Installment Agreement, you have 30 days in which to file the appeal, and you receive this same protection during that time period. Incidentally, a managerial hearing is not required when filing a CAP on the denial or termination of an Installment Agreement.

If you are appealing a seizure action, you have 10 days in which to file a CAP.

Note that sometimes you may be entitled to both a CDP hearing and a CAP hearing for the same notice. However, the IRS only permits you to file one, not both. If you need the time provided by the CDP, then file that one. If you are looking for speedy resolution, look to the CAP program.

In most cases, Appeals is required to hear your and make a determination within 5 days. CAP appeals are the highest priority item in the Appeals universe. During this 5 day period, levy action is stopped if it hasn't been already due to other legal requirements on the government, as mentiond above. The exception to this rule is if Collections personnel believe that the CAP is being filed in order to delay levy action for no other purpose than to prevent collection. For example, people have filed CAP appeals in the past in order to give them a couple days to move money out of the country, or to drain accounts into cash so that the government can't seize it. The IRS calls this a "jeopardy" case, because they think collection is in jeopardy. In these cases, levy action will likely continue.

If Appeals decides in your favor, then Collections is required to act immediately upon that decision. It also goes the other way, however, and Collection action will resume if Appeals sides with the Collections division, unless the 30 day rule mentioned earlier for Installment Agreement denials and terminations applies.

The CAP program can be a great tool for obtaining immediate relief from overly aggressive collections action by the IRS. The program definitely requires that you have all your "ducks in a row" in order to obtain a favorable outcome.

Trust Fund Recovery Penalty Assessment Appeals

The Trust Fund Recovery Penalty (TFRP) is a penalty issued against an individual for failure to pay to the government the income tax, Social Security, and Medicare taxes withheld from employee's paychecks at a business. The TFRP, also referred to as a "6672 penalty" due to the section of the Internal Revenue Code from which it comes, is an administrative (non-court ordered) piercing of the corporate veil.

The IRS will generally attempt to assess the TFRP against anybody it thinks it can. While there are defined procedural requirements for issuing a Letter 1153 that actually proposes the assessment against you personally, it is not uncommon in my experience for a Revenue Officer to skip these procedural requirements and just assume that all business owners or officers should be assessed and send the notice.

In order to successfully appeal a TFRP assessment, it is important to understand exactly who, under the tax code, this penalty can actually be assessed against. In order to be imposed with the TFRP, you must be determined to be **both** "willfull" and "responsible" for not having paid the government the trust fund taxes from the business operations.

In other words, in order to be "responsible", you had to have been the person who's job it was to make Federal Tax Deposits (FTD). You can be considered responsible if it was at all a part of your position within the company, even if it was normally physically done by somebody else. If you have never been in any way responsible for or involved with handling payroll and tax matters at your company, then you have a very solid argument against being "responsible".

Similarly, even if you were "responsible" for making tax payments, the IRS must demonstrate that you "willfully" chose not to. Even if making tax deposits is entirely your job at the company, but you do not have signature authority over the bank account to spend the company's money, and somebody else at the company prohibits you from using company money to make the tax deposits, then that other person is "willfull" in not making the payments.

I have seen tax cases where the TFRP fell entirely upon a company employee, such as a bookkeeper, that wasn't even an owner or officer. This was because the bookkeeper had signature authority over the bank accounts to spend the company's money, and was fully responsible for handling payroll and tax matters, but because cash flow was tight for the business, chose to pay rent, utilities, payroll, etc., in order to keep the business operating, instead of paying taxes.

I have also seen cases where the TFRP fell upon nobody at the company, because one person was responsible, and another person willfull. For example, a small business operated by a husband and wife team could be set up such that one spouse does payroll and handles tax returns, but has no signature authority over the bank account. The other spouse has to sign every check, authorize every expenditure, etc., and it can be clearly demonstrated that the other spouse never has and never will have authority to spend money. In this case, one person is responsible, and the other is willful, but neither person is both, so neither of them is assessed the TFRP.

If the IRS is coming after you for the TFRP of a business that you either work for or own, then professional representation is often highly advisable. However, you can appeal the proposal yourself using either a Small Case Request or a Written Protest.

A Small Case Request is used if each and every one of the proposed penalty amounts, on a per tax period (usually quarter) basis, is less than $25,000. A Written Protest is required if any single tax period exceeds $25,000.

A TFRP appeal is handled by your local Appeals office, and is filed with the person proposing the assessment of the TFRP against you, who then forwards your appeal to the Appeals division.

The major difference between a Small Case Request and a Written Protest is that the Written Protest must be signed under penalty of perjury, whereas a Small Case Request does not.

There is no IRS form for filing this particular type of Appeal. Instead, you should write a letter that includes the following information:

1. Your name, address, and Social Security Number.

2. A copy of the Letter 1153 you were sent.

3. A direct statement saying you want an Appeals hearing.

4. A list of the tax periods you are appealing.

5. A statement explaining why you are not responsible, willful, or both. Specifically, explain your duties, authorities, and responsibilities at the company, and why these make you not responsible or not willful.

6. For a Written Protest, your last paragraph should state:

"Under penalties of perjury, I declare that I have examined the facts presented in this statement and any accompanying information, and, to the best of my knowledge and belief, they are true, correct, and complete."

Like other Appeals types, you'll receive a letter back from Appeals acknowledging your request, and scheduling a hearing and perhaps requesting other supporting documentation to prove your case.

Penalty Abatement Denial Appeals

If a Revenue Officer or Service Center Penalty Appeals Coordinator denies your request for a penalty abatement, that denial comes with Appeals rights.

When filing an appeal of a penalty abatement denial, do the following:

1. Write a letter back to the person that denied your penalty abatement requesting that your request be sent to Appeals for reconsideration.

2. If you have already paid the penalty, include a Form 843, Claim for Refund, for each tax period you are requesting penalty relief for.

3. Include a copy of your original written request for penalty relief, and a copy of the denial letter.

Appeals consideration of penalties has an additional interesting possibility other than full abatement; Appeals has the authority to settle penalties for less than what is owed, without going through the Offer in Compromise process. Due to the fact that an Appeals denial of penalty relief comes with the right to sue the Federal government, and Appeals is required to consider the possible of the government having to spend money to defend itself in court, Appeals is granted the authority to settle penalties for less than what is owed based on the potential risk of litigation.

In other words, threatening to sue over your penalties may actually be to your benefit.

ABOUT THE AUTHOR

Jasssen Bowman is a Federally licensed taxpayer representative in private practice. He currently represents individuals and small businesses with complex IRS issues. He also deals extensively with international tax matters, particularly with American expatriates that live abroad in Asia and Australia. As a leader in the field of tax resolution, he also provides training to other tax professionals to increase their competency in this challenging tax practice specialty.

Jassen takes on a limited number of new clients throughout the year. If you owe the IRS at least $50,000 and would like a case review, please visit www.TaxHelpHQ.com and click on "Request Case Review" to download a case review questionnaire to complete and submit. You may also reach his office by calling (970) 930-1040.

www.ingramcontent.com/pod-product-compliance
Lightning Source LLC
Chambersburg PA
CBHW060614200326
41521CB00007B/774